JOSEPH

The Journey to Forgiveness

A Bible Study by

Melissa Spoelstra

Abingdon Women
Nashville

JOSEPH: THE JOURNEY TO FORGIVENESS

This book is printed on elemental chlorine-free paper.
ISBN 978-14267-8910-6

All Scripture quotations, unless otherwise indicated, are taken from the *Holy Bible*, New Living Translation, copyright © 1996, 2004, 2007. Used by permission of Tyndale House Publishers, Inc., Carol Stream, Illinois 60188. All rights reserved.

Scripture quotations marked NIV are from the Holy Bible, New International Version®, NIV®. Copyright © 1973, 1978, 1984, 2011 by Biblica, Inc.™ Used by permission of Zondervan. All rights reserved worldwide. www.zondervan.com. The "NIV" and "New International Version" are trademarks registered in the United States Patent and Trademark Office by Biblica, Inc.™

Scripture quotations marked "NKJV"™ are taken from the New King James Version®. Copyright © 1982 by Thomas Nelson, Inc. Used by permission. All rights reserved. All scripture quotations, unless otherwise indicated, are taken from the New King James Version®. Copyright © 1982 by Thomas Nelson, Inc. Used by permission. All rights reserved.

Scripture quotations marked RSV are taken from the Revised Standard Version of the Bible, copyright 1952 [2nd edition, 1971] by the Division of Christian Education of the National Council of the Churches of Christ in the United States of America. Used by permission. All rights reserved.

Scripture quotation marked NASB is taken from the New American Standard Bible®, Copyright © 1960, 1962, 1963, 1968, 1971, 1972, 1973, 1975, 1977, 1995 by The Lockman Foundation. Used by permission. (www.Lockman.org)

15 16 17 18 19 20 21 22 23 24 — 10 9 8 7 6 5 4 3 2 1
MANUFACTURED IN THE UNITED STATES OF AMERICA

Contents

About the Author

Melissa Spoelstra is a popular women's conference speaker, Bible teacher, and author who is madly in love with Jesus and passionate about studying God's Word and helping women of all ages to seek Christ and know Him more intimately through serious Bible study. Having a degree in Bible theology, she enjoys teaching God's Word to the body of Christ, traveling to diverse groups and churches across the nation and also to Nairobi, Kenya, for a women's prayer conference. Melissa is the author of *Jeremiah: Daring to Hope in an Unstable World*. She has published articles in *ParentLife*, *Women's Spectrum*, and *Just Between Us*, and she writes a regular blog in which she shares her musings about what God is teaching her on any given day. She lives in Dublin, Ohio, with her pastor husband, Sean, and their four kids: Zach, Abby, Sara, and Rachel.

Follow Melissa:

Twitter	@MelSpoelstra
Instagram	@Daring2Hope
Facebook	@AuthorMelissaSpoelstra
Her blog	MelissaSpoelstra.com (check here also for event dates and booking information)

Introduction

Do you ever find your mind replaying old tapes of wrongs done to you? Have you walked into a room, spotted someone who has hurt you in some way, and wanted to walk the other direction and hope the person didn't see you? Maybe your pain runs deep from fresh wounds, or perhaps old scars leave a daily reminder of discomfort from the past. All of us know what it's like to feel betrayed by someone we trusted. Often it's a small breach such as being overlooked, hearing a demeaning comment made about you, or being neglected in a time of need. Other times we've experienced lies, gossip, or harsh words that cut us to the core. Some of us have endured unspeakable pain through abuse, adultery, or abandonment.

Someone in your life has hurt you, whether he or she meant to or not. Sometimes we are the victim while other times we are the perpetrator. When someone says words that can't be taken back, behaves badly in moments of anger, or hurts us through action or inaction, we can find ourselves reeling from the blows. God knows the pain we cause each other and longs to help us learn to practice forgiveness.

This Bible study was born out of my own struggle to forgive. God teaches us through His Word the dangers of unforgiveness. In Hebrews 12:15 we read, "Look after each other so that none of you fails to receive the grace of God. Watch out that no poisonous root of bitterness grows up to trouble you, corrupting many." Bitterness becomes a poisonous cup that cripples us when we continue to drink from it, paralyzing our relationships, our thought life, and even our faith. The consequences of holding on to the hurt inflicted by others can ruin the way we view God, ourselves, and other relationships. The stakes of forgiveness are high, and when betrayal gets personal in our lives, it certainly isn't easy.

As I've battled to make sense of pain in my life, I've asked questions such as:

- Where do I start? How do I stop dwelling on things said or done to me?
- How do I tame my emotions and thought patterns in order to see my offender through God's eyes?
- Is it ever okay not to forgive? Does it cheapen justice to forgive, especially when the wrongdoing is abusive, murderous, or truly evil?
- When will I stop having to re-forgive? Will I ever just be "over it"?
- What is the difference between forgiveness and reconciliation? Is it possible to forgive without reconciling?
- What about trust? Does forgiveness mean I let others repeat offenses without setting boundaries?

Nowhere do we see forgiveness played out more fully in Scripture than in the Genesis account of Joseph. No sugarcoating there. Forgiveness rises to the top in this story, but not without the messy grappling with grace that we all encounter. During the next six weeks we will open the text of Genesis 37–50 to explore what God has to say in our lives through Joseph's story of trial and triumph. As we study his dreams, betrayers, dysfunctional family, struggle to forgive, and journey toward reconciliation, we will find truths that echo into our own situations.

Options for Study

As we begin our journey to forgiveness alongside Joseph, it will be important to decide what level of commitment our time and life circumstances will allow. I have found that what I put into a Bible study directly correlates to what I get out of it. When I take time to do the homework daily instead of cramming it all into one sitting, God's truths sink deeper as I have more time to reflect and meditate on what God is teaching me. When I am intentional about getting together with other women to watch videos and have discussion, I find that this helps keep me from falling off the Bible study wagon midway. Also, making a point to memorize verses and dig deeper by looking at additional materials greatly benefits my soul.

At other times, however, I have bitten off more than I can chew. When our faith is new, our children are small, or there are great demands on our time because of difficult circumstances, ailing parents, or other challenges, we need to be realistic about what we will be able to finish. So this study is designed with options that enable you to tailor it for your particular circumstances and needs.

1. Basic Study. The basic study includes five daily readings or lessons. Each lesson combines study of Scripture with personal reflection and application (boldface tan type indicates write-in-the-book questions and activities), ending with a suggestion for talking with God about what you've learned. On average you will need about twenty to thirty minutes to complete each lesson.

When you gather with your group to review each week's material, you will watch a video, discuss what you are learning, and pray together. I encourage you to discuss the insights you are gaining and how God is working in your own life.

2. Deeper Study. If you want an even deeper study, there is an optional "Read Through Joseph's Family Story" challenge that will take you through Genesis 12–50 to help provide both context and continuity for your study of the Joseph narrative in the final fourteen chapters of the book. Watch for the prompts in the margins. Additionally, Digging Deeper articles are available online (see www. AbingdonPress.com/Joseph) for those who would like deeper historical context about Joseph's family, Egyptian practices, and structural nuances in the text that lend fuller insight. Finally, memory verses are also provided for each week of study so that you may meditate on and memorize key truths from God's Word.

3. Lighter Commitment. If you are in a season of life in which you need a lighter commitment, I encourage you to give yourself permission to do what you can do. God will bless your efforts and speak to you through this study at every level of participation.

Take some time right now to pray and decide which study option is right for you. Then fill in the circles below to indicate which aspects of the study God is calling you to complete. Be realistic, but also allow yourself to be stretched and challenged as the Holy Spirit directs.

O   Make the group sessions a priority. Watch the video and engage in discussion and group learning.

O   Complete as much of the homework as you can between sessions.

O   Complete all five days of homework between sessions.

O   Memorize the memory verse(s) (one to two verses for each week of lessons).

O   Take the "Read Through Joseph's Family Story" challenge, which will guide you in reading through Genesis 12–50 over the course of the study.

O   Read the additional Digging Deeper articles found online that give additional insights and information on related topics.

Be sure to let someone in your group know which parts of the study you plan to do so that you have some accountability and encouragement.

A Final Word

As we delve into Joseph's story and lift the lid on our own forgiveness stories from the past or present, we might find some pain resurfacing. Perhaps you have completely forgiven someone, but simply remembering the situation brings up hurtful memories. A resurfacing of pain doesn't mean we haven't forgiven; it only indicates that our memories include emotions as well as facts. We will learn more about this in our study. Or perhaps you understand the need to forgive but are looking for God's help and guidance as you struggle to find peace in letting go of offenses. No matter what has been done to harm you, God wants to free you from the chains of unforgiveness and bitterness. He calls you to find freedom as you release your pain to Him so that He may do a supernatural work of forgiveness in your life. In fact, He wants to use the very things intended to hurt you for your benefit. This is the God we serve. He exchanges beauty for ashes (Isaiah 61:3), raises up life out of dry bones (Ezekiel 37:4-6), and uses even our most painful circumstances as a source of blessing in our lives.

You may be thinking, *I don't really have anyone to forgive right now.* While we aren't always working through a betrayal or hurt, we do rub shoulders with other sinners in our homes, churches, and communities. Even if you can't relate with the need to forgive at this moment, God might want to prepare you and grow you for future opportunities to forgive. As you study Joseph's story, I pray you'll get to know your forgiving God better. Jesus modeled ultimate forgiveness by giving His own life on our behalf.

We can't do it on our own. We desperately need God's Spirit and Word to help us sort through fact and fiction so that we can make the journey to forgiveness. It will mean getting real, raw, and possibly reopening some painful memories. But the freedom and healing on the other side will be well worth it as we search the Scripture alongside others who want to become more like Christ, learning to extend the same grace and forgiveness they have received from Him. As we finish our six weeks of study, I pray that we will be able to take Joseph's posture toward those who hurt us, saying, "You intended to harm me, but God intended it all for good" (Genesis 50:20a).

Week 1

ACKNOWLEDGING THE PAIN

Genesis 37, 39

I pour out my complaints before him
  and tell him all my troubles.
When I am overwhelmed,
  you alone know the way I should turn.
                    (Psalm 142:2-3)

Fun Fact:

Joseph's name means "May God add" or increase (Genesis 30:24).

Day 1: A Dysfunctional Family

We don't have to look much farther than our own front door to find a place to practice forgiveness. Living in close proximity to others provides many opportunities to hurt one another. With pretenses down, we unveil our true selves at home. Family members see what we hide from others outside our four walls—such as laziness, selfishness, anger, and favoritism.

I've heard it said that the true test of a Christian is how he or she lives at home. Families are the people committed to love us even when our flaws are exposed. Whether through birth, adoption, or the covenant of marriage, family connections often involve our closest relationships: husband and wife, parent and child, sister and brother, grandparent and grandchild.

What family member are you closest to at this stage in your life?

Now imagine the pain if that person was disloyal to you in some way. When that sacred trust is broken, the betrayal cuts deep wounds. Carrie* said this about the fracture in her family:

How do I forgive someone who stood before God and a church full of people and vowed to be faithful until death but then deceived, lied to, and manipulated not only me but also our children and everyone we both knew in order to hide his adulteries? He then manipulated church leaders into believing I was crazy. When finally the truth was revealed and he was confronted by a pastor, he confessed. After hearing what he would have to do to redeem the situation, he packed and left. He vowed to destroy me and turn my children against me. He did everything he could to fulfill that vow even to the spiritual destruction of the children. He threw away everything we had spent years building, along with the future of enjoying family gatherings, weddings, grandchildren, and a spouse in old age. How do you ever forgive that person?

*Apart from documented sources, all names of those who have shared their stories have been changed.

I've known many other women like Carrie who've experienced excruciating betrayal by a family member. Joseph's story of betrayal also begins at home. Actually, all of us grew up in a dysfunctional family because no family is perfect.

What are some memories of family experiences or situations that have given you the opportunity to forgive—whether recent or long ago?

Let's learn a little bit about Joseph's family so that we can understand better the nature of dysfunction in his home. I assure you that it will help you feel better about the problems in your own family. Someone asked me recently why the biblical accounts are so full of things such as polygamy, rape, murder, and all sorts of moral failures. While I've asked that same question myself, I have come to believe that one reason is to give us hope that God can work amidst our own messy lives.

Circle Joseph in the family tree below:

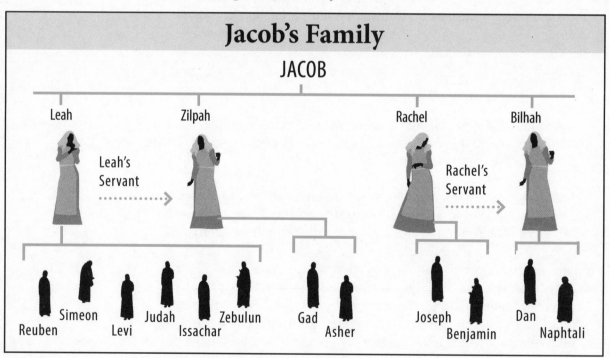

Jacob's Family

JACOB

Leah   Zilpah   Rachel   Bilhah

Leah's Servant

Rachel's Servant

Reuben   Simeon   Levi   Judah   Issachar   Zebulun   Gad   Asher   Joseph   Benjamin   Dan   Naphtali

How many women bore children to Joseph's father, Jacob?

To understand the extent of the family drama that we will explore in our weeks of study, we need to look back at the soil where the roots of discord began to grow in this family, beginning with Jacob's family of origin. (We find the details in Genesis 27–30.) Though Jacob was his mother's favorite, his father, Isaac, had a special affinity for his twin brother, Esau, which left Jacob with a father wound. Jacob not only stole the birthright from Esau, the firstborn, but he also tricked his father into giving him the blessing intended for Esau by dressing up as his twin brother. Esau wasn't very happy with his brother's deceit and threatened to murder him. So Jacob fled to his uncle, Laban, who lived far away, and immediately he fell in love with his cousin Rachel (literally on his first day in town—the moment he laid eyes on her). We learn that right after he watered Rachel's flocks, "Jacob kissed Rachel, and he wept aloud" (Genesis 29:11).

Jacob worked for his uncle for seven years in order to marry Rachel, and on the day of their marriage he was tricked at the altar, waking up in the morning to find Rachel's older and less attractive sister, Leah, under the wedding veils. The Scriptures put it delicately when contrasting the two girls: "There was no sparkle in Leah's eyes, but Rachel had a beautiful figure and a lovely face" (Genesis 29:17). Some translations say that Leah had "weak eyes."

When Jacob expressed his unhappiness over being tricked into marrying the sister with "weak eyes" (NIV), he was given Rachel as well at the end of her sister's bridal week with his promise to work for Laban for seven more years.

According to the family tree, how many children did Leah give to Jacob? 6

Who was Joseph's mother? Rachel (Also Benjamin)

Now, two other women bore Jacob children in this story. When Rachel struggled with infertility at first, she gave her servant Bilhah to Jacob so that she could have children through her. Though Leah bore Jacob many sons, she also later gave her servant Zilpah to Jacob to increase her status through having more children.

The people who followed God during the times of the Patriarchs viewed children as gifts from the Lord. More babies meant more blessings. Social status and greater security came to the woman who bore many children because the children would provide for their mothers when they got older. With the dangers of infant death, illness, and war exponentially higher for this group of people, the more sons to take care of you the better. Infertility brought grief not only for a woman's unrealized maternal instincts but also through the scorn of others who often equated the inability to have a baby with God's punishment.

When Rachel finally gave birth to Joseph, he entered the world into a family feud between two sisters seeking status in different ways. Rachel, though favored by her husband, felt shame in her barrenness. Leah attempted to compensate for her "weak eyes" and the lack of her husband's love with many sons. Jacob, the head of the household, suffered from the lack of his father's approval and the loss of his mother's presence in his life (after fleeing his homeland), so he looked to soothe his pain in the arms of a woman.

Are you starting to feel that your family's problems aren't so unusual after all?

Read Genesis 37:1-4. According to verse 3, why did Jacob favor Joseph? *Because he had been born to him in his old age*

What did Jacob give to Joseph as a sign of his special favor? *A richly ornamented robe*

Knowing a little of the family history, can you think of any other reasons why Jacob might have favored Joseph? *He was the son of Rachel whom he loved dearly*

Joseph's birth had ended a long season of infertility for Jacob's beloved wife, Rachel. Jacob didn't hide his favoritism toward Rachel's firstborn. One would think Jacob might have understood the pitfalls of preferring one child over another after the debacle of his own parents' favoritism (Genesis 25:28). Even when bad behaviors and their consequences are modeled for us, we too can struggle to keep history from repeating itself.

Take another look at Genesis 37:1-4. How did the brothers know that Joseph was their dad's favorite?

According to verse 4, how did Jacob's favoritism affect the brothers' relationship with Joseph?

Did you grow up in a family where you felt that one sibling was favored over another? If so, where did you fit into the scenario?

What would you say are two damaging consequences of favoritism that you have experienced firsthand or learned from watching others?

1.

2.

Jacob wasn't aware of the extent of damage he was inflicting on his family by overtly favoring one child over the others. As parents, we would do well to be on guard against comparing our children or bestowing special favor on one. While things will not always seem completely fair in our children's eyes, we must diligently make a concerted effort to make each one feel special and loved.

My husband and I often take our children on individual outings. These are special getaways from the craziness of everyday life to be intentional about understanding their joys and fears by asking them questions and valuing them with our time and attention. At times we've kept track of these dates on a chart so that they know when their turns are coming. I can't imagine if we were to practice this with only one child. The others certainly would feel left out.

Now, try for a moment to put yourself in Joseph's shoes. Though I'm sure he enjoyed the blessing and affection of his father, he went out to the fields sometimes with his brothers. Meals and holidays likely were spent together as well.

As a seventeen-year-old boy, what mixed feelings do you think Joseph might have had about his position in the family?

As I was growing up, I often was teased as being the favored child. When the four kids wanted to make a plea to our parents, I was sent to negotiate. From my siblings' point of view, my consequences seemed to be less and my benefits appeared to be more. Whether some of this favor was merely perceived, it left me in a strange position at times. While I enjoyed the good relationship I had with my parents, the disdain from my brother and sisters wasn't fun at all.

I wonder if Joseph ever wanted to take off his special coat when he was around his brothers or apologize for his special gift. Perhaps as a seventeen-year-old he sometimes paraded around, showing off his favor, while other times he regretted the loss of sibling camaraderie. In any case, that coat came to represent both the love of his father and the growing hatred and envy of his brothers, which we will see compounded in tomorrow's lesson.

When you watch others receive unfair favoritism, what initial feelings come to the surface?

This week we are going to find that the first step on the journey to forgiveness is acknowledging the hurt. We can never forgive without getting honest about our pain. Joseph's brothers endured some unfair neglect because of a birth order they had no control over. Whether they intended to or not, Jacob and Joseph inflicted wounds on the brothers. And the brothers had the choice of working toward forgiveness or vengeance. While you may not be struggling with being on the wrong end of favoritism as Joseph's brothers were, it's likely that you are carrying some pain at the expense of others.

Who has contributed to the hurt you are currently feeling?

What does that pain look like in your world right now? In other words, how are your thoughts, emotions, attitudes, and actions affected by the actions or inactions of this person or persons?

Today we've looked at the first milestone on the journey to forgiveness. Rather than sweeping our feelings under the rug or pretending we aren't hurt, it is important to acknowledge what we feel. Ultimately, we cannot forgive without acknowledging the offense.

Talk with God

You keep track of all my sorrows.
You have collected all my tears in your bottle.
You have recorded each one in your book. (Psalm 56:8)

Tell God how you feel about whatever hurt you have identified. He saw ... He longs to listen and talk with you about it. He has collected ... hurt to the One who cares more than anyone ... you.

e Fire

... him in his business. The ... her, worshiped at the same ... places such as Europe and ... e vacations and many other ... s began to change in their ... up late, miss meetings, and ... spoke to John regularly about ... overlook as much as he could ... ration began to mount among ... ey eventually banded together ... eration with John was so great ... ot let go. After much wrestling ... , hoping that by not working ... ing their friendship. Yet things ... hip after John left the company. ... ily seek to sort through the facts, ... oes by that Mark doesn't ponder ... such a great rift to come between ... t have done differently.

I, too, have felt the sting of ... dship and have questioned myself about what part I played in contributing to my own friends' problems. If we have played a role in creating the circumstances that have led to our injury or betrayal, are the others involved still to be held accountable for what has happened? If we have been provoked by another person, can we excuse our reaction? These are the kinds of practical questions that often torment us. Clarifying who and what warrants forgiveness is vital in our journey toward healing.

Yesterday we explored some of the bad blood between Joseph and his brothers. What are some of the reasons you recall that Joseph's brothers "couldn't say a kind word to him" (Genesis 37:4)?

Fun Fact:

The original meaning of the Hebrew word for Joseph's coat "is 'a coat of extended length,' literally, a coat that extends to the hands and feet." It wasn't until the ancient Greek translation of the Jewish Scriptures (the Septuagint, also known by the Roman numeral acronym LXX) when the coat is referred to as colorful.[1]

Today we delve into Joseph's behavior to see if he added any fuel to the fire of his brothers' hatred, and we will consider how forgiveness applies when we've played a part in a conflict.

Read Genesis 37:1-11 and fill in the chart below, noting what each party said or did to the others:

Brothers	Joseph	Jacob
v. 4	v. 2	v. 3
v. 8	vv. 6, 9	vv. 10, 11

I sometimes wonder why details are left out in the biblical text. I want to know exactly what the brothers did that led Joseph to report on them. Was it a major offense, such as harming the sheep or stealing? Or was Joseph overzealous and getting them in trouble for taking too many work breaks or neglecting some minor shepherding procedure? When things aren't clear in a passage, it causes us to search and interact with God to discern truth from His Word. First Corinthians 13:12 assures us that one day we will have all the details: "Now we see things imperfectly, like puzzling reflections in a mirror, but then we will see everything with perfect clarity. All that I know now is partial and incomplete, but then I will know everything completely, just as God now knows me completely."

Though I'm glad that one day we'll get the full story, for now I have some questions about this part of the story:

- Should Joseph have tattled?
- Should Joseph have shared his dreams in the manner that he did?
- Was he guilty of fueling the fire of jealousy?

What are some other questions you have regarding this passage?

What questions do you have about how you might be contributing to the friction related to a strained situation in your own life?

Some scholars maintain that Joseph shouldn't have shared his dream. "Even if the dream came from the Lord, it was for his own encouragement,

not for their edification, and he was very unwise to insist on telling it to them."[2] Other commentators disagree: "Perhaps Joseph might have been more diplomatic in the way he reported his dreams, but surely he was right in sharing them with the family."[3] While the dreams came from God, perhaps Joseph communicated them insensitively. We don't apologize for our dreams, job promotions, or exciting news, but we must be careful to show tact when choosing with whom and how we share them.

Can you think of some situations when it might be inappropriate to share exciting news with a particular audience? Explain below.

We need to be mindful even with good news. An infertile couple will want to hear of a dear friend's pregnancy, but the news must be shared thoughtfully. A recently unemployed sister might find it difficult to celebrate her sibling's promotion. We must be careful to use discernment and tact in our words so that we do not add fuel to the fire of their pain unintentionally.

Now let's return to the question of the part Joseph played in the conflict. Let's assume that Joseph wasn't completely innocent in his behavior. Does this mean he deserved what he got?

Read Genesis 37:12-37 and summarize below how the brothers took vengeance into their own hands:

Do you think Joseph's brothers were responsible for their actions even though Joseph could have contributed to their jealously and hatred with his bad report against them, his favored status with their father, and his dreams that clearly put him in authority over them? Why or why not?

This is an important question that impacts how we forgive. Let's consider a quick scenario of three friends.

Sally: Sally is really upset when word reaches her that her good friend Mary has broken a confidence by sharing private details of her life with others. In a moment of pain she dials Mary's number and speaks accusatory words for minutes on the phone without

asking any questions or allowing a response. Then she hangs up on Mary.

Mary: Mary feels hurt and upset by the phone call and believes Sally jumped to conclusions without having all the facts. She hasn't broken Sally's trust and wants to sort things out, but now she is offended by the way Sally handled the situation.

Jane: Jane loves both friends and has only heard Sally's side of the story. So she confronts Mary and learns about the phone call. However, she believes Sally shouldn't be held responsible for her actions because she wouldn't have behaved badly unless she had been really hurt by what she'd heard. She believes the two friends should wipe the slate clean, pretending none of it ever happened. No one needs to admit, apologize, or forgive—just rewind the clock and start over.

What is your response to Jane's conclusion? Explain your answer.

Sally, Mary, and Jane's scuffle may be small scale, but little things can blow up when gasoline is poured on embers. I've seen it happen, and sadly, the clock cannot be rewound. Whether the situation is small scale or far more serious, the question at the heart of the matter is this: Should one person's pain, whether it is real or perceived, justify poor reactions? Can a combustible situation be extinguished rather than inflamed?

Did Joseph get what he deserved? Some might say that if Joseph had been more humble and his father had showed less favoritism, the brothers wouldn't have had a reason for vengeance; therefore, they could not be held responsible for what they did because they were just victims of their circumstances. But the truth according to God's Word is that we cannot claim innocence for our bad decisions because someone did something to provoke us.

Joseph's brothers had a legitimate right to feel pain. Their perception of Joseph's haughtiness, his dreams to rule over them, and their father's favoritism left them angry. They also may have been afraid. In those days, the firstborn son received the birthright. But Leah's firstborn, Reuben, disqualified himself by sleeping with Bilhah (one of his father's concubines). Simeon and Levi, the next in line, led a murderous attack on Shechem without their father's approval, which left them out of their father's good graces. Though there were still seven brothers who were older than Joseph, they might have feared that Joseph was weaseling his way into the position of power in the family. Because Rachel was supposed to have been Jacob's first wife, it could be argued that her firstborn should have been the next patriarch of the family. Joseph's dreams would only have intensified this fear.

Even so, the brothers could not excuse their wicked behavior with these reasons. They certainly knew what God said about murder and revenge. Without television, computers, video games, or shopping malls, the way to pass the hours on evenings and trips was often storytelling. All of the Genesis stories prior to their own story would have been passed down orally. The story of Cain and Abel would have been familiar to them, and they would have known very well how God felt about murder (see Genesis 4). Living in close quarters and taking journeys together in their nomadic way of life, they would have heard about the character of God through the stories of His relationship with their father Jacob, their grandfather Isaac, and their great-grandfather Abraham. Joseph's brothers could have acknowledged their hurt and their hate and then asked God to help them heal. Instead they took vengeance into their own hands.

We, too, have a choice of which posture we will take when legitimate hurt comes into our lives. Which will we take: *a victim mentality*, seeing ourselves at the mercy of our pain, or *a victor mentality*, acknowledging the hurt while seeking God's help in pursuing healing?

How have you struggled with these two internal postures?

What helps you move from victim to victor in your heart and mind when you are struggling with pain?

Even if another person fans the flames of our pain, God calls us to forgive rather than excuse ourselves to disobey His commands.

I've heard my children make excuses like these:

- "I wouldn't have hit her if she hadn't kept annoying me."
- "I wouldn't have thrown a fit if she had given me back my iPod."
- "I would have done my work if she hadn't been singing so loud that I had to leave the room."

They have come up with some good ones. Like other children, they don't want to be accountable for what they've done when they believe someone else pushed them to it. We can be much like children,

Even if another person fans the flames of our pain, God calls us to forgive rather than excuse ourselves to disobey His commands.

excusing our wrong choices because we had our embers stoked until we allowed ourselves to burst into flames.

Can you think of a situation in which you are choosing to overlook your part in a conflict because of another party's wrong behavior? (Think about relationships in your family, work, church, and community.) Describe it below.

It's always our turn to do the right thing for the right reasons. Forgiveness isn't one option on a list of possible choices for followers of Jesus; it is the only way to peace and freedom.

Talk with God

Spend a few minutes in God's presence, asking Him to help you sort through the muddle of your relational circumstances. Ask for clear vision to see any course correction you need to make so that you don't end up like Joseph's brothers—throwing someone out of your life in retribution. (We may not toss someone into a physical pit, but we are skilled at edging people out emotionally and socially to punish them when we feel wounded.) Make notes in the margin of any action steps God is calling you to make in order to put out a potential relational fire.

Day 3: Taming the Wild Horses

Over thirty years ago, Pam's husband had an affair with her best friend. She felt kicked in the stomach emotionally, which left her physically ill with migraine headaches. She felt spiritually knocked down as well since she didn't anticipate this from her husband, who was a traveling minister at the time. Fresh tears came to her eyes as she recalled the pain even though she had long ago traveled the difficult road to forgiveness. Her honesty touched me as she remembered her best friend stoking the fires of hurt while she battled to forgive and re-forgive with each new offense. At one point she even wanted to kill her former friend when she thought of the harm her friend was causing her daughter by feeding her lies that eventually landed her daughter in therapy.

Though we might not want to admit the thoughts we've had about those who've seriously hurt us, the truth is that most of us have wished some severe pain on our betrayers. After we have acknowledged the depth of our hurt, we also must be real about the emotion of hate.

I don't like the word *hate*. In his book *Forgive and Forget*, Lewis Smedes writes, "The act of forgiving, by itself, is a wonderfully simple act; but it always happens inside a storm of complex emotions. It is the hardest trick in the whole bag of personal relationships."[4] In the book he outlines what he refers to as the four stages of forgiving:

1. Hurt
2. Hate
3. Healing
4. Coming Together

Smedes says, "If we can travel through all four, we achieve the climax of reconciliation."[5]

As I read his book, I wanted to protest number two. Hate seems like such a strong word. *Can't I just feel dislike toward someone who has harmed me?* I wondered. However, the more I have pondered, prayed, and studied forgiveness, the more I have come to believe that Smedes is right. Pain causes powerful emotions in our lives. Though we may not spew our anger in an outburst, our hate may take more passive forms as we silently wish bad things for those who have hurt us, pray imprecatory prayers for them, or let our anger leak out in passive-aggressive comments. If you are having trouble with the word *hate*, then perhaps you will acknowledge that negative emotions often follow pain in our lives.

If we don't acknowledge our negative emotions, we can't move on to the next step of healing. A friend of mine shared with me how she taught her daughters from a young age about their emotions. She said emotions are like wild horses who want to jump, kick, and make loud noises. In order to tame the wild horses within, we can't stuff our feelings. They will break out one way or another. Instead, we must get honest in front of God and others about the emotions that betrayals or hurtful actions unearth in us and ask God for help.

Lewis Smedes tells the story of a woman who came home early from the gym to find her husband and the teen girl they'd recently taken into their home in a compromising position. She said this of her feelings: "Are you supposed to swallow hard, let him off the hook, and pretend the whole thing never happened? If that is what forgiving is about,...I would rather buy a gun and shoot them both."[6] She grew up in the church and knew she was supposed to forgive, but she was surprised at the power of the wild horse within when she came face-to-face with betrayal.

Describe some wild horse emotions you have struggled to tame when you have felt betrayed or wounded:

Fun Fact:

Joseph's father, Jacob, was about ninety years old when Joseph was born.

Read back through Genesis 37:4-11 and note below some of the emotions Joseph's brothers felt toward him:

What circumstances led them to feel these strong emotions toward Joseph?

Even if Joseph egged them on with his coat, his tattling, and his recounting of dreams of ruling over them, the brothers' wound took root in the perceived lack of favor from their father. Yet Joseph wasn't to blame for being born to his father's favored wife or for being the object of his father's special attention. In the haze of our emotion, we too can easily find an inappropriate target for vengeance.

When we hurt, it can lead to hate or other negative emotions such as jealousy, anger, and greed. Unless we acknowledge the hate and ask God to help us heal, we will turn toward fleshly responses and ride the wild horses of emotions until we get bucked off.

What are some natural human reactions to betrayal that you have experienced in your own life or observed in the lives of those around you—before asking God to do His supernatural work of healing?

Bitterness and the need for vengeance can consume us when we reel from the hate and envy we carry inside. When I asked Pam how she was able to let go of bitterness and her desire for vengeance, she said she eventually became so miserable and unhappy that she knew she had to find freedom or she would die. She thought, *I can't live like this; it's just too painful.* So she began her journey to forgiveness, releasing the hatred and anger inside of her. Though it didn't happen overnight, she knew she had no choice except to forgive. She couldn't ride the wild horses of hate much longer if she wanted to survive. Pam found healing in turning to God and getting honest about her hurt and hate.

As we saw yesterday, Joseph's brothers did not tame their wild horses but rode out their desire for vengeance. Review Genesis 37:12-36 and answer the following:

Though the text does not state it explicitly, Joseph's brothers would have had time on their journey to Shechem to brood and commiserate together about the unfairness of their plight.

When an opportunity for vengeance presented itself to the brothers, they did not hesitate to act. What was their original plan when they saw Joseph in the distance? (v. 18)

What stopped them from carrying out this plan? (vv. 21-22)

Even though Joseph's brothers ultimately chose not to murder him, you could say that they reacted strongly to his dreams! It should not surprise us that the brothers reacted so strongly. After all, they had a history of struggling to control their passions. As we learned yesterday, Reuben, the oldest, demonstrated his lack of restraint and slept with his father's concubine Bilhah (Genesis 35). Likewise, Simeon and Levi demonstrated wild horse emotions when they slaughtered the men of Shechem to the embarrassment of their father (Genesis 34). Judah, as well, would soon prove himself to be a man struggling with self-control when he picked up a temple prostitute who turned out to be his own daughter-in-law (Genesis 38).

These were not men who had a great track record of restraining their emotions and passions. So when the brother who reminded them of a deep father wound appeared on the scene, they defaulted to their natural, fleshly tendency and took vengeance into their own hands.

Are there hurts from your past that still sting when you recall them? If so, name them below.

Have you ever taken even small steps of vengeance? If so, how did it feel in the moment? How did it feel later?

What do the following verses tell us about a few of the negative emotions that Joseph's brothers acted on?

Proverbs 10:12

Matthew 5:21-22

1 John 2:9

Fun Fact:

"The Hebrew word for 'dreamer' implies one who is a master at dreaming, perhaps suggesting that he is good for nothing else."[7]

Digging Deeper

This week we are covering Genesis 37 and 39. Are you curious about what happens in Genesis 38? Check out the online Digging Deeper article for Week 1, "A Story within the Story," to find out how this chapter diverges from the Joseph narrative to give us some additional insight into the life of his older brother Judah (see AbingdonPress.com/Joseph).

At times we all feel negative emotions toward persons who hurt us, so what are we to do with those emotions? We have options just as Joseph's brothers had. We can

- Dwell on the emotions and let them fester inside.
- Take steps of vengeance against those we perceive to be the source of our pain.
- Ask God to help us heal.

Sometimes we do all of these. The tough question is, *Where do we start when we want to heal but the wild horses won't stop thrashing about in our hearts and minds?* Joseph's brothers chose vengeance, which led to other negative decisions such as covering up the crime with lies. But we can make a different choice. As we will see in the weeks to come, Joseph learned to tame his wild horses. I pray you'll remain open to how God wants to work in your life as we learn how he was able to take his hurt and hate to God and find healing.

Talk with God

Let's end our time in God's Word today by talking with God about our pain, so that we don't follow in the footsteps of Joseph's brothers. Tell God about anything that is causing you pain, whether it is a fresh wound or an old scar that itches from time to time. Acknowledge the pain and ask Jesus to help you forgive, re-forgive, or simply tame the wild horses of emotion that you feel toward the individual(s). Now watch God begin His healing work as you continue this practice of acknowledging your feelings and relying on God for help.

Day 4: The Before and the After

An old friend called to tell me she realized her life can be summed up in two categories: before and after. A few years ago Cindy and her family underwent a very painful time when her pastor husband was fired from a large church. The devastation could fill a book. They lost not only her husband's job but also their church family and community; what had been close friendships now were complicated. I've heard it said, "There is no pain like church pain." That has certainly been true for my friend. Although much time has passed and they now serve a new church, have many new friends, and can see God at work in their hearts, some things can trigger Cindy to revisit the pain of the past. When her daughter reconnected with a friend at Vacation Bible School and asked to invite her over, Cindy felt her heart race as she realized that this was the daughter of a man who served on staff at the church that had fired her husband. In fact, Cindy's husband had recommended him for the job, and he had played a significant role in the church conflict. Although the man's wife probably had nothing to do with the situation, the thought of speaking to her about a playdate reopened the old wound.

Joseph could have divided his life into the same two categories: before and after his brothers betrayed him. I can only imagine seventeen-year-old Joseph in the bottom of that pit. We find out later in Genesis 42:21 from the brothers' own words that Joseph was distressed. "We saw his anguish when he pleaded with us, but we would not listen." Did he apologize for telling on them or for flaunting his father's favor? Did he quietly cry, wondering how in the world to reconcile the dreams God had given him with what appeared to be impending death at the hands of his own brothers?

Joseph went from hero to zero in a very short time. He was not dead, but neither was he free. He was now living in the uncertainty of what his future would hold.

Can you relate to such a great loss? You may not be dead, but you certainly don't feel free. You have no idea if relief and justice will come in the next day, month, or year—or not at all. It's a scary place to be.

The roller coaster of circumstances turned Joseph's perfect world as the preferred son with a beautiful robe and dreams of greatness to a scared boy at the bottom of a pit with a very uncertain future.

Although Judah persuaded his brothers to sell rather than kill Joseph, what thoughts and emotions do you think Joseph might have had as he was taken by foreigners along the road to Egypt?

Imagine the confusion of not understanding the foreign language spoken by his captors. For a boy who lived a sheltered life under his father's protection, fear of the unknown would have been bad enough, but it's likely that betrayal at the hands of his own flesh and blood was even worse, topping the list of crimes committed against him. The reality of the turn of events changed everything in Joseph's life.

In Charles Dickens's famous novel *Great Expectations*, Miss Havisham encounters this kind of day when her fiancé leaves her jilted at the altar. She lives out the rest of her days wearing her bridal gown, with every clock in her house stopped on the moment she got word of the betrayal. The cake begins to rot on the table while Miss Havisham's dress becomes tattered and faded. She lives only to inflict her pain on those around her. She never recovers from the day the clocks stopped in her life.

Have you ever experienced a moment when your world seemed to change in an instant? Perhaps you learned of the betrayal of a friend or spouse or the death of a loved one. Maybe you expected a promotion only to leave your boss's office bewildered by the news of termination. Or perhaps you've experienced emotional, physical, or sexual abuse. Like my friend Cindy, you may have wounds that divide your life into before and after.

Have you ever had an experience that left you feeling much like Joseph along the road—alone, terrified, hopeless? Does any particular day or event come to mind? If so, briefly describe it below.

My friend Cindy and I talked about how we would not have had an answer for that question five years ago. If you are in that boat, just tuck these truths into your heart and mind. Though I hope a day never comes when the clocks stop in your life, the truth is that at one time or another most of us will have some kind of hurtful experience, perhaps of betrayal, that divides our lives into before and after. One of my before and after moments revolves around how planting a church has impacted our family and friendships. For my daughter with alopecia, she divides her life into before and after she lost her hair. Your pain might seem to pale in comparison to some of the things that others go through, but remember that even the smallest offense can begin to consume us if left unchecked—unforgiven.

While we may never be able to make sense of the devastation that often invades our lives when we least expect it, we can find glimpses of hope in the midst of our despair just as Joseph did. His clocks didn't stop forever like Miss Havisham's. Instead, he found a road to healing even while living in captivity.

Read Genesis 39:1-6 to learn what became of Joseph after his world turned topsy-turvy. How many times does the word LORD appear in these verses?

How did the LORD show up in Joseph's life even during his time of captivity?

During a difficult time, how have you experienced God's nearness and favor even in the midst of your pain?

Whether or not God has given us a specific dream about our future as He gave to Joseph, most of us have had dreams or ideas about our future that did not turn out the way we expected. Would you say your life has played out the way you imagined it would when you were a high school student? Explain your response.

None of us starts out in life hoping for these things:

- I hope to endure a messy divorce.
- I hope to have strained relationships with family members.
- I hope to have an unfair boss who doesn't appreciate my work.
- I hope my friends will betray me and gossip behind my back.
- I hope my church leaders will offend and confuse me.

When we hover at a low point and nothing seems to be working out the way we thought it would, God remains faithful.

Yet often our dreams and reality do not connect very well.

Joseph probably didn't think his dreams were connecting with reality either. However, we see from the text that the Lord was with Joseph even when nothing made sense in his life. And Joseph had eyes to see God's favor. As one source notes, "This is not a story of the success of Joseph; rather it is a story of God's faithfulness to his promises."[9] The good news for us is that when we hover at a low point and nothing seems to be working out the way we thought it would, God remains faithful.

As we sort through the Joseph narrative, one danger is to try to make a connection between Joseph's behavior and God's favor. Though the Bible tells us in general terms that God rewards obedience and disciplines us when we get off course (Psalm 19:9-11; Proverbs 3:11-12), we cannot determine how that works out in our lives or the lives of others. It can be dangerous to play god and draw sharp cause-and-effect lines in our circumstances. Yet often when things go wrong, our tendency is to search for the source of the problem. When we get cancer, have wayward children, or are betrayed by someone we trusted with our heart, a warped mind-set can cause us to look for a reason why calamity has knocked at our door. And it breaks my heart when some Christians respond to a tragedy by calling the victim to search for the source of sin and repent. It's not cause and effect.

Hebrews 11 gives us a clear picture of saints who encountered great success and others who endured horrifying situations.

Read Hebrews 11:32-38 and answer the following questions:

What were some of the amazing things people accomplished through faith? (vv. 32-35)

What were some of the terrible things that happened to others who had faith? (vv. 35-38)

What does verse 38 say about those who suffered?

> *God never leaves us and even draws nearer to us in our times of desperation.*

Some people of faith saw incredible miracles, and others faced devastating circumstances. God doesn't say that we will never face betrayal or tragedy, but He does promise to be with us through it. Deuteronomy 31:6 tells us, "Be strong and courageous. Do not be afraid or terrified because of them, for the LORD your God goes with you; he will never leave you nor forsake you" (NIV).

No, God wasn't punishing Joseph for bad behavior by allowing his betrayal. And God wasn't rewarding Joseph with favor in Potiphar's house because of good behavior. God doesn't withhold trials when we are "good" and bring them when we are "bad." Regardless of our circumstances, God remains faithful. When the clocks stop in our lives, His compassion is great. God never leaves us and even draws nearer to us in our times of desperation.

As head of Potiphar's household, Joseph was still a captive—bought and paid for by Potiphar. He must have missed his family and friends and the familiarity of his food, language, and culture. Yet he recognized God's favor even in the "after" of his life. We can too.

My friend Cindy saw God's favor when the other mom came to pick up her child from the playdate. Anxiety rose inside her as the clock revealed an encounter approaching with a woman whose husband had caused much grief for her whole family. What would she say? Could she really be nice?

"God, please help me," she prayed. God answered with a puppy. You see, Cindy is the biggest puppy lover you will ever find. She can't help but smile and laugh and speak baby-doggy talk in their presence. And as the mom walked toward Cindy, she was carrying in her arms their brand new

> *Fun Fact:*
>
> *At the time of Joseph, Egypt was a land of superstition, with more than two thousand gods and goddesses and an emphasis on preparing for the afterlife.[10]*

puppy. Instead of an uncomfortable moment, Cindy was able to show genuine puppy love and see walls coming down in the process.

God wants to walk with you through every step of the "after" moments in your life, too. He longs to bless each of us and show us His favor in unique and incredible ways. He can even use a puppy to make things easier for us! Watch for His blessings today!

Talk with God

Whether you are living in the "before" or "after" of some difficult event or time in your life, take a moment to count the blessings from God that you've seen just this week. Has He provided for a financial need? Has He given you grace to deal with difficult people? Has He prospered your work? Did He bring some relief from physical pain? Like the psalmist, take this posture: "My eyes strain to see . . . / the truth of your promise fulfilled" (Psalm 119:123). God is faithful. Ask Him to give you eyes to see His favor through the haze of hardship.

List at least five things you can attribute to God's faithfulness in your life right now. (I think that puppy would be on the top of Cindy's list!)

1.

2.

3.

4.

5.

Day 5: Run for Your Life

When my son was in seventh grade, he transferred from the private Christian school he'd been attending since kindergarten to our local public school. He was a shy kid who wanted to fly under the radar without drawing much attention while he navigated new waters. Imagine his surprise the first month in his new school when he was called to the principal's office and told someone had reported him for inappropriate texting on his phone. My son didn't even own a phone, and so he defended himself as best he could.

Read Through Joseph's Family Story:

Read Genesis 16.

Fun Fact:

Joseph lost a garment each time he was betrayed. His brothers took his robe or coat (Genesis 37:23), and Potiphar's wife took his cloak or shirt (Genesis 39:12).

I called the principal the next day to be sure he wasn't still suspect, wanting to satisfy my sense of justice for a wrongful accusation. She assured me that she had quickly learned it was a case of mistaken identity with another student in his homeroom who had the same first name. Thankfully, the situation was resolved easily, but that's not always the case with false allegations, is it?

Have you ever felt wrongfully accused? Whether someone assumed your guilt, maliciously lied about you, or subtly implied your wrongdoing, what was it like to be accused of something you didn't do? Write two adjectives to describe your situation (or how you think you would feel if this ever happened to you):

_____

_____

Unfair and _calculated_ are two words that came to my mind. Our sense of justice really emerges when people are wrongfully accused—especially when it's us. The few times I've felt unjustly accused, I've experienced these desires:

- To defend myself and provide evidence to prove my innocence.
- To bring up the faults of my accuser.
- To write passive-aggressive comments about the situation on social media.
- To tell others my side of the story.

I try to refrain from following through with these urges, but I must admit that they are my first thoughts when I am blamed for something that I do not believe is my fault.

Joseph endured temptation that culminated in a wrongful accusation that would serve as a second major betrayal in his life. It was another moment when the clocks could have stopped in his life. Let's read about the incident.

Read Genesis 39:6-9 and make some notes in the chart on the next page about each person—his or her appearance, attitude, character, or anything else you notice.

Potiphar	Potiphar's wife	Joseph

These aren't characters in a musical about a Technicolor dreamcoat. They were flesh-and-blood people with desires such as those we have today.

According to some commentators, Potiphar might have been castrated. The text refers to him as a word that is often translated "eunuch." In Egyptian culture, many Pharaohs feared a takeover of their dynasty, so they had their most prominent leaders become eunuchs so that they could focus more on their jobs and refrain from the temptation for a coup.[11] In any case, we know from the text that Potiphar's wife began to see Joseph as an object of her desire.

When Potiphar's wife propositioned Joseph, what three reasons did Joseph give as to why he couldn't comply with her request? (vv. 8-9)

1.

2.

3.

Joseph was a man. He had physical desires. I'm sure he struggled with temptations to give in to what feels good in the moment instead of what ultimately pleases God. He might have rehearsed these three reasons to himself many times and meditated on them so that he wouldn't give in to his flesh. Potiphar's wife treated Joseph like property; he became an object to her. But even though she propositioned him day after day, he continued to maintain his integrity.

What do you think are some things Joseph might have done in order to repeatedly make the wise choice when faced with the same temptation?

Have you ever been bombarded with the same temptation again and again? Check all those that apply, and add another if you want:

___ To cut corners at work
___ To have an inappropriate relationship
___ To feed a food, alcohol, or sexual addiction
___ To keep "ingesting" inappropriate television, books, or magazines
___ To be disrespectful to someone
___ To _____

When we are bombarded by temptation, what can we do to stay true to what we believe—even at the risk of our job, our friends, or our very lives?

Read Genesis 39:10. What does this verse say that Joseph did *specifically*?

Yes, he stayed as far away from Potiphar's wife as possible!

There was a time when I was struggling with how social media was affecting my thought life. It was reopening old wounds and causing me to view things that triggered old resentments. God called me to stay off of social media for a few weeks and keep my focus on Him. So I deleted a few apps from my phone and decided I would reinstall them only when I was in a better frame of mind.

What is it for you? It may be that you need to steer clear of friends who tempt you to engage in gossip, or avoid that coworker who tends to flirt, or minimize contact with a neighbor who doesn't understand some new dietary choices you feel God calling you to make. Whatever it is, God may be calling you to avoid temptation in order to maintain your integrity and keep growing in faith.

Take a moment to get quiet and listen to God. Where do you sense someone feeding your temptation to sin in an area that you are trying to overcome?

Joseph loved and forgave those who hurt him, but he had healthy boundaries when needed, as we will see throughout his story.

Running can be a mark of a coward, but sometimes God calls us to flee. The Apostle Paul wrote, "Flee the evil desires of youth and pursue righteousness, faith, love and peace, along with those who call on the Lord out of a pure heart" (2 Timothy 2:22 NIV). God also might call us to flee a toxic relationship, a compromising job, or a spiritually abusive relationship or group. While we can't run away from every problem, there is a time when God says the best thing to do is get out of Dodge.

Sandy found this to be true for her when some friendships that once had been healthy and encouraging began to turn in a different direction. The exclusivity and gossip she fell into when she was with those friends wasn't honoring God and was stifling her spiritual growth. God called her to set some boundaries in the relationships, but she fought it. It seemed disloyal, and she thought it would be perceived as judgmental to communicate that she could no longer attend certain exclusive gatherings. So Sandy put it off, sought godly counsel, prayed and fasted, and asked God to help her see another way out. Still, He said she needed to flee. It wasn't easy, and things did seem to go from bad to worse after she put some distance in the relationships. But in the "after," Sandy learned a lot about forgiveness and putting God first in everything.

Staying focused on God's truth rather than human desire cost Joseph greatly. It led to a second betrayal, which took him from his initial captivity as a slave in Potiphar's house to a much worse imprisonment. Things went from bad to worse for Joseph, which raises a question: If God's hand of favor was on him, as we read yesterday, why did all of these bad things happen?

Just as we can't sort out all the reasons for the difficult circumstances in our own lives, we don't know for sure why these bad things happened to Joseph. However, from the perspective of hindsight, we can see some benefits to Joseph's trials.

Warren Wiersbe writes, "Had he stayed home with his pampering father, Joseph might not have developed the kind of character that comes from hard work and obeying orders. God's method for building us is to give us a job to do and people to obey. He tests us as servants before He promotes us as rulers."[12] Sometimes you have to learn to follow so that you can lead.

Joseph's great grandfather Abraham received a promise from God that we refer to as the Abrahamic Covenant, found in Genesis 12:3: "All the families on earth will be blessed through you." Joseph brought this blessing with him even as a slave. While we don't get too many glimpses into Joseph's thoughts and feelings, we do see a boy becoming a man as God blesses his administration of Potiphar's house. Joseph lives out Proverbs 22:29: "Do you see a man who excels in his work? / He will stand before kings; / He will not stand before unknown men" (NKJV).

God wants us, like Joseph, to recognize His favor so that we can focus our eyes on blessing others rather than sitting in our self-pity for all the wrongs done against us. The opportunity to serve others and work hard can become God's gifts to help us on the journey to forgiveness.

Now let's finish Genesis 39 and end our week acknowledging God's faithfulness in the midst of the pain of life's betrayals.

Read Genesis 39:19-23 and write one sentence describing how God remained faithful to Joseph even when things went from bad to worse in his life:

*Sometimes you
have to learn to
follow so that
you can lead.*

God continues to bless us even when we feel like we can't sink any lower. He is crazy about us! While we can't always make sense of the whys and hows of what we're enduring when others hurt us, we can rest assured that God will never leave us or forsake us.

Think back over all you've learned from Joseph's life this week about acknowledging pain in difficult circumstances. Write one or two key statements or concepts that stuck out to you in your time of study:

Talk with God

Spend some time in prayer, praising God for the favor He has shown you even in some very low times of life. Pray for those who have wrongfully accused you in the past and for anyone who has truly betrayed you. Acknowledge the pain they have caused you. Remember that Joseph didn't cover up the hurt or pretend it didn't happen. Likewise, we can't move on to the healing until we acknowledge the hurt and other emotions we feel.

Ask God to give you eyes to see what your response should be to the things you can't control in your life. Write a short prayer in the margin.

Acknowledging the Pain

The first thing we have to do is _____ our feelings.

Even if we feel guilty, God is greater than our feelings, and he knows everything. (1 John 3:20)

We need Jesus to help us _____ the fire of pain.

A gentle answer deflects anger,
        but harsh words make tempers flare. (Proverbs 15:1)

We have to leave _____ in God's hands.

Dear friends, never take revenge. Leave that to the righteous anger of God, for the Scriptures say,

"I will take revenge;
        I will pay them back,"
        says the Lord. (Romans 12:19)

If we don't forgive the _____ stuff, it turns into _____ stuff.

When you walk through the fire of oppression,
        you will not be burned up;
        the flames will not consume you. . . .
Others were given in exchange for you . . .
because you are precious to me. (Isaiah 43:2b, 4)

Week 2

WAITING TO BE REMEMBERED

Genesis 40

Memory Verse

Look after each other so that none of you fails to receive the grace of God. Watch out that no poisonous root of bitterness grows up to trouble you, corrupting many.

(Hebrews 12:15)

Day 1: Keeping the Dream Alive

As I sat in a cute little tearoom, I listened to a friend recount her story of pain. She had taught Bible studies, blogged, and led in the women's ministry at her local church. Leading, writing, and speaking energized her as she felt equipped and called of God to use her gifts to serve others. After a series of misunderstandings, a group of women's ministry leaders asked her to step down from her position of teaching.

She questioned herself, wondering how things had come to this and exactly how she was to use her God-given gifts. After some time to process and pray, she humbly asked the women's leaders for a path back into ministry. They confirmed her call and her ability as a teacher and gave her constructive feedback. However there was no place for her to teach in women's ministry at that time. As we sat having tea several months later, she was still waiting for the path back to become clear. When I asked her how she felt now in a ministry lull, she replied, "I feel like Joseph in prison, waiting to be remembered." She knew God had called her to women's ministry and has plans for her, but right then she could do little else but wait.

As we pick up Joseph's story this week, we find him stuck in prison, waiting for his God-given dreams to come true with no evidence that things will change anytime soon. How could he continue to hope and also process his new opportunity to forgive after being falsely accused by Potiphar's wife?

What emotions and thoughts do you imagine Joseph would need to process in prison?

Perhaps it was difficult to realize that the boss who had been so impressed with him was now furious with him for something he didn't do. Could Joseph also have wondered why God allowed more unfair treatment? Hadn't he had his fair share of rejection and injustice at the hands of his own brothers? Why would God allow additional injustice?

Fun Fact:

Dreams played a very important part in the life of leaders in Egypt, and the ability to interpret dreams was a highly respected skill.

That day as we talked over tea, my friend mentioned that feeling as if you are in prison is different than times of wandering. Prison walls cause you to feel that you can't go anywhere. At least when you are wandering, the scenery changes from time to time.

Think about your life. Is there any area in which you are waiting for change? Is there a relational conflict that isn't fully healed? A situation that never seems to get better? A move or job change that is looming but clear direction still hasn't come? Write below one area in your life where you are waiting for something to happen:

If you aren't in a season of waiting right now, think of a time in the past when you were waiting. Check one of the following, or write your own:

___ To get married

___ To have a baby

___ To find a friend

___ To get the right job

___ To fulfill a dream

___ To _____

In your current or past experience with waiting, what thoughts and feelings have you experienced when it seems like nothing will ever change?

During periods of waiting and isolation such as Joseph experienced, we have much time to think and process our circumstances. These are days when bitterness is knocking on our door, bidding us to nurse unforgiveness and build walls to keep others out. Let's pick up Joseph's story where we left off last week to see what was happening during his days of waiting.

Read Genesis 40:1-23 and look for details about Joseph's season of waiting. Note any observations or questions that come to mind as you read this passage:

Did you notice the glimmer of hope for a change when Joseph asked the cupbearer a question? What did Joseph ask him to do? (v. 14)

I wonder if Joseph woke up with anticipation the day after the cupbearer was restored. Did he convince himself that maybe it would take a week or two to get the balls of justice rolling? At some point, he must have realized that the cupbearer wasn't going to come through for him. Joseph's hopes of getting out of prison seemed to be dashed.

Perhaps Joseph was angry at the cupbearer for forgetting him. In the soil of reflection, seeds of bitterness can grow strong roots as we rehearse the wrongs done to us. The reality for Joseph and for us is that we can't control some events in our lives.

Joseph had no control over being chosen as his father's favorite, betrayed and sold by his brothers, bought by Potiphar and elevated in rank, tempted by Potiphar's wife, falsely accused and imprisoned, and forgotten by a man he had helped. We too have things in our lives that we wish were different but we have no power to change. Some of them for me right now are that one of my daughters has alopecia (she has no hair and wears wigs) and a water pipe burst under our house, causing us to use all of our tax refund for a not-fun project.

Now think about your life. What are some difficult things that you have no control to change right now?

Though Joseph could not change some of his circumstances, he did have control over his response to those events. Let's look at a few of Joseph's difficulties again.

Look up the following Scriptures, and write a word or phrase describing Joseph's response to each event:

Scripture	Event	Response
Genesis 39:8-10	Tempted daily by Potiphar's wife	
Genesis 39:20-23	Falsely accused and imprisoned	
Genesis 40:5-8	Sees prisoners looking dejected	

Joseph couldn't control his circumstances, but he could govern his own spirit. Though initially he may have flaunted his father's favoritism, he learned to work hard, honor God, and maintain integrity even during his time of captivity. Proverbs 25:28 says, "Whoever has no rule over his own spirit / is like a city broken down, without walls" (NKJV).

Of course, Joseph was human, just as we are. I'm guessing he had to work through the hurt and the hate. However, he was able to move toward healing and right responses as evidenced by his attitude of concern for the baker and cupbearer. If he had lingered in his own personal pity party, he probably would not have been able to help the two prisoners he encountered. As we see with other biblical characters, God is more concerned with Joseph's character than with his comfort.

I find that the same holds true in my life. God seems more concerned about my character than He is about my comfort. Can you relate?

In our times of waiting, God prepares us for new beginnings. Whether they are big or small, we all have realities that we can't change in life. Like Joseph, the only variable we can control is how we will choose to respond to these events and the people involved in them. Will we maintain our integrity when no one is looking? Will we choose joy even when our circumstances go from bad to worse? Will we posture ourselves for forgiveness or vengeance?

Look back at your list of difficult things in your life that you can't control. How will you choose to respond to these things? Write an attitude, action, or posture that you can control related to each item on your list:

Jack Canfield uses this formula to explain the concept of responding to events beyond our control:[1]

$$E + R = O$$
(Event + Response = Outcome)

The events in our lives that we can't control, plus the attitudes, actions, and words we use to react to those events, equal the outcomes. We only get a choice in one variable in this equation, and that is our response.

Now let's apply this principle to those who have hurt us. In a world full of sinners, including you and me, we fail each other all the time either by something we say or something we do, or perhaps by our inaction.

Think of a couple of recent offenses against you, whether they are heavy on your heart or just little things weighing on the corners of your mind. Think of two situations with two different people (you can't list the same person for both). Complete the chart, noting how you responded to each offense:

Read Through Joseph's Family Story:

Read Genesis 18.

Who did it?	What did the person do or fail to do?	How did you respond?

Like Joseph, we have no control over the wrongs done to us. Friends can neglect us, neighbors can choose to gossip about us, husbands or friends can betray us, and children can speak cutting words to us. (Anyone else have teenagers?) At times, all we can control is our response. In the fire of an offense, our flesh beckons us to lash back or retreat in bitterness; but God calls us to bring our hearts to Him for supernatural healing. In her book *Choosing Forgiveness*, Nancy Leigh DeMoss writes, "God does not want you to run *away* from your pain but to run to *Him* in the *midst* of your pain—to fly head-on into the full fury of it, to face it, to let Him meet you right where it hurts and give you the grace to be set free from any bondage to that hurt."[2]

It is possible to be free. You don't have to stay in the prison of unforgiveness and bitterness, which is far worse than the dungeon where Joseph served out his undeserved sentence. Joseph discovered the secret of a soft heart and the power of forgiveness in the midst of great betrayal. As we continue to study Joseph's life, I pray we will see his humanity and the reality of his pain coupled with the ultimate freedom he found in a close relationship with his God. We serve the same Lord who enabled him to respond to his betrayers with grace. God can do the same for us as we start our own journey toward forgiveness.

Talk with God

If you are in a time of waiting, ask God to soften your heart and identify any areas where you might have seeds of bitterness taking root. Ask Him to reveal areas of unforgiveness that need to be brought to light.

If you are not in a season of waiting right now, take some time to pray for someone you know who is experiencing such a season. Ask God how you might encourage and love this person through a time when it's hard to keep dreams alive.

While reading numerous books on the topic of forgiveness, I noted that several authors mentioned a book titled *The Sunflower: On the Possibilities and Limits of Forgiveness*. Intrigued by the mention of a story from World War II, I devoured this account of a Jewish man named Simon Wiesenthal living in a Nazi concentration camp. One day on a work assignment at his old high school, which had been turned into a makeshift hospital, Simon was summoned by a nurse to come into a patient's room. He found himself with a dying young German soldier who was explaining some terrible acts he had committed. This soldier followed orders alongside his peers to round up Jewish families into a building where the doors were locked and then set on fire. Ordered to shoot anyone who jumped from the second story, this eighteen-year-old man, wrapped in bandages and struggling to breathe, desperately pleaded with Simon to forgive him for participating in the tragedy. His conscience left him in more agony than his wounds. Simon walked away without saying anything. He could not relieve this man's pain while living his own nightmare under Hitler's regime in a Lemberg concentration camp.

After surviving the war, Simon spent the rest of his life pondering what he should have done in that moment. This event became his before-and-after story. Should he have granted forgiveness? Was it even in his power to offer such a thing? Theologians, rabbis, politicians, and people from many different backgrounds wrote responses to his question with mixed responses.

What about you? How would you respond to Simon's question of whether he should have forgiven the Nazi soldier? Explain your response.

Joseph's story brings to the surface some tough questions: Does choosing to forgive condone injustice? Are some sins unforgivable? Are we always to forgive, even when someone takes part in truly evil actions?

As Joseph languished in prison, was he giving up on justice if he forgave his brothers and Potiphar's wife? Does forgiving someone condone his or her terrible behavior? If someone whose son was murdered or whose daughter was abused asked you these questions, how would you answer?

These are hard questions. I want to camp in Genesis 40 this week because I believe the prison years in Joseph's life are critical. It is in such times of waiting and darkness where we make secret choices of the heart and mind that shape how we act and speak later.

Read again Genesis 40:14-15 and write what Joseph said about the things that had been done to him:

It's important to note that Joseph acknowledged he had been mistreated. He told these two royal servants that he had been kidnapped and had done nothing to deserve imprisonment. Though ultimately Joseph forgave the ones who kidnapped and sold him, he never said that what they did was okay. This distinction is of great importance.

Forgiving someone doesn't excuse or minimize the pain that the person has caused, and often consequences remain for those who have sinned against us. It is possible to forgive others and still hold them accountable for their behavior. We can forgive others while speaking up about their actions and asking for help in seeking justice on our behalf.

I sometimes find in Christian circles that speaking up about wrongs done to us and asking for justice is equated with a lack of forgiveness. However, the two are not mutually exclusive. We can speak up and ask for help in righting the wrongs committed against us while simultaneously working through the stages of forgiveness.

We've already seen that a first step to forgiveness is acknowledging our pain. Let's take a closer look now at the steps of speaking up and asking for help.

Speaking Up: "I Don't Deserve This!"

Joseph wasn't some doormat of a man who let others walk all over him without speaking up. He did not condone or make excuses for his brothers' behavior or his wrongful imprisonment. Rather, he told the two royal servants that his sentence was unfair and that he did not deserve the consequences he was facing daily in prison. In verse 15 he said basically, "I don't deserve this!"

Of course, we need the discernment and guidance of the Holy Spirit in order to know when and how to speak up—whether we are to speak up to ourselves (in our own minds), to others, or directly to those who have wronged us. Later in our study we will learn that there is a time to be quiet and let God fight our battles, as well as situations when love is to cover sin. Our faithful God walks with us intimately to help us discern both when to speak up and to whom our words should be directed. However, we do learn from Joseph's words to the baker and cupbearer that there is a time to speak up about unfair treatment.

When we have been mistreated, betrayed, abused, or sinned against in any way, it's okay to say: "This wasn't right, and I didn't deserve to be treated in this way." In fact, if we excuse behavior rather than calling it sinful and wrong, we inhibit forgiveness from actually taking place. Lewis Smedes explains it this way: "Forgiving is tough. Excusing is easy.

What a mistake it is to confuse forgiving with being mushy, soft, gutless, and oh, so understanding. Before we forgive, we stiffen our spine and we hold a person accountable. And only then, in tough-minded judgment, can we do the outrageously impossible thing: we can forgive."[3]

Forgiveness doesn't negate the wrongness of a crime but, instead, readily admits that wrong was done. Pardon isn't necessary if sin wasn't committed. Simon Wiesenthal might not have been able to forgive the soldier that day for many reasons. First of all, the crimes were not committed against him. How could he speak for the families and friends of those who were burned to death in the house that day? He also needed time to process and discern through the haze of hunger, mistreatment, and injustice in his own life. Forgiveness of atrocities requires time. If it happens too quickly, one might question the sincerity and depth of it.

Part of prospering in our prisons means sorting through wrongs done to us. As you think about ways you are suffering the consequences of what others have done to you—whether parents, friends, co-workers, or strangers who got close enough to harm you personally—it's okay to say, "I don't deserve this."

Finish the sentence below:

I don't deserve _____.

Asking for Help: "Get Me Outta Here!"

Joseph did something else that I often struggle to do. He asked for help.

Look again at Genesis 40:14. Write the two things Joseph asked of the cupbearer:

1.

2.

First, Joseph asked for the cupbearer to remember him and show him kindness. This is a request for pity—for the cupbearer to understand his pain. Joseph had been falsely accused, and he asked for kindness, or compassion. The Hebrew word used here, *hesed*, is the same word we find in Genesis 39:21: "The LORD was with him; he showed him kindness and granted him favor in the eyes of the prison warden" (NIV). God was showing Joseph kindness in prison, and Joseph was asking for kindness from a flesh-and-blood human who might be able to help him. One authority notes, "For all his reliance on God, Joseph must depend on the act of a covenantal neighbor."[4] Even though Joseph trusted God, he still communicated his need in the moment.

Joseph not only asked for emotional understanding but also for specific steps to be taken. He asked the cupbearer to tell Pharaoh about his situation so that he could get out of prison. Pharaoh was the highest authority in Egypt and even was worshiped as a deity, and Joseph had no reservations about going straight to the top with his problem. He thought his circumstances were worth mentioning to the highest authority in the land.

When we are in our own prisons of waiting and are feeling unjustly treated, we need to be willing to ask for help as Joseph did. I'm sure Joseph bent God's ear many times, pleading for a way out. He also appealed to someone around him who might be able to help—the cupbearer.

What did Joseph and the cupbearer have in common?

Like Joseph, the cupbearer had been wrongly accused and was now serving an indefinite prison sentence. Both dreamed of good things that were not yet realized. The fact that the cupbearer would be restored also meant that he might have the opportunity to speak on Joseph's behalf.

Many of us suffer in silence. We isolate ourselves, thinking no one understands our situation. Though our trials are unique and no one else has our exact circumstances, we can follow Joseph's example and open our eyes to see others around us in somewhat similar situations.

As you consider your current opportunities to forgive, are there others around you who have experienced similar things? Perhaps you need God to show you others whose

- husbands have been unfaithful to them.
- parents have abandoned or abused them.
- children have disappointed them.
- friends have hurt or betrayed them.
- employers have been unfair to them.
- medical diagnosis has limited them.
- neighbors have spoken harshly to them.

If your particular need is not included in this list, write it here:

Whatever hurtful situation you are experiencing, look around you in your time of waiting to see if there is someone you can share your burden with, and then ask this person for help. Whether you need compassion or a specific action to be taken on your behalf, follow God's Spirit in taking steps to ask for it. The purpose of asking for help is not to share your viewpoint to get people to join your side of a conflict. When we truly want to grow in forgiveness, we are not looking for what I call "puppy licking"—in other words, people who will mindlessly stroke us and tell us we are always right. We need compassion but also wisdom and truth. So we must exercise good judgment in asking for help from someone we respect. Did this person learn through his or her trials? Will this person be a good example that we would want to emulate? Proverbs 12:26 says, "The righteous choose their friends carefully, / but the way of the wicked leads them astray" (NIV).

In the space below, write the name of someone who would be safe to share your burden with—someone to whom you could make an appeal for compassion and understanding:

In times when I have been burdened or hurting and have needed help from a trustworthy friend, I have humbly

- texted friends and asked for prayer for specific struggles or thoughts.
- asked some mentors to watch my life, attitude, and responses to specific situations and let me know if they see signs of pride or bitterness creeping in.
- picked the brain of other moms about how to handle difficult parenting situations.
- e-mailed a friend for advice about business situations.

Ask God to reveal if there is anything tangible you can ask the person whose name you wrote to do to help you through your current "prison"—whether it is emotional, physical, mental, or spiritual. Write below anything the Holy Spirit brings to mind:

> *"Keep on asking, and you will receive what you ask for. Keep on seeking, and you will find. Keep on knocking, and the door will be opened to you."*
>
> *(Matthew 7:7)*

Proverbs 28:1 tells us, "The wicked flee though no one pursues, / but the righteous are as bold as a lion" (NIV). Joseph was bold as a lion. He learned to speak up and ask for help. Joseph's plea for help didn't bring change immediately. As we learn in Genesis 41:1, it was two years before the cupbearer remembered Joseph to Pharaoh. Yet Joseph's request ultimately led to a turn of events that changed the entire course of his life.

Read Matthew 7:7 in the margin and summarize the main idea in one sentence:

Whether your answer comes in two weeks, two months, or two years, you can speak up and ask for help as God leads. Though it may seem that those you ask are not being helpful, keep waiting. Trust that God will release you from your prison cell at just the right moment.

Talk with God

Ask Jesus to show you where and how He is calling you to boldly speak up and ask for help. Spend some time in His presence, letting His love wash over you as you realize that His purpose in your waiting might be to prepare you for a new beginning.

Day 3: Discerning Through the Haze

During our prison seasons, when we feel the walls closing in on us, we are forced to process the events that landed us in a dark place. Louis Zamperini knew what prison life was like. His story, told by Laura Hillenbrand in the book and 2014 movie titled *Unbroken*, follows Louis's life as a young Olympic runner who became a B-24 bombardier when World War II broke out. When his plane was shot down, he barely survived on a life raft for over forty days until being captured by the Japanese. As a prisoner of war in enemy territory for over two years, he went through many difficult days. One particular Japanese camp guard that the soldiers nicknamed "the Byrd" was especially cruel to Louis. I could barely stand to read about the inhumane atrocities he endured.

Louis's strong spirit got him through. However, he discovered that readjusting to life outside prison walls was not as easy as he anticipated. He found himself lost in the haze of what he had experienced. His hatred for the Byrd became so intense that he could think of little else than plotting his revenge. He looked for ways to get back to Japan to hunt him down and kill him. His marriage and sanity teetered on the brink of survival as he was plagued by his memories and fantasies. His unforgiveness no longer belonged to him; he was held captive by his desire for vengeance.

While we don't know much about Joseph's incarceration years from the Genesis account, a few more details are afforded us in the psalms.

Read Psalm 105:17-22 and label the picture with what was found on Joseph's neck and feet:

Fun Fact:

The job of a cupbearer was to prepare and taste Pharaoh's wine because poison would be a convenient way to begin a coup and grab power in Egypt.

Ultimately, Joseph became the warden's favorite and was put in charge of other prisoners (Genesis 39:21-22). However, at some point he truly suffered physically. The iron collar on his neck and shackles on his feet served as tangible reminders that his slavery had reached a new level with the accusation of Potiphar's wife. His loss of freedom was as clear as the fact that he couldn't turn his own neck or take one step without a heavy weight.

Though our shackles may not be made of iron, we still may walk in pain from the wrongs done to us. We need God's help to process our pain so that we can see clearly. Our thoughts and emotions can run so wild that our perception of the facts becomes distorted. Mental and emotional caution is required so that bitterness and revenge don't take root and skew our view of reality.

I have both experienced and observed that pain can distort how we interpret situations, attitudes, or words. Here are some tendencies I admit that I can relate to:

- When someone we once looked up to hurts us, we quickly switch tracks from idolizing to demonizing the person. Though we once saw everything about this individual as good, we now see everything he or she does as bad.
- We judge others by their actions, but we judge ourselves by our intentions. We draw conclusions about someone's motives with our own reasoning.
- "Balloons" grow in our heads from the smallest things. We read into an intonation, gesture, or comment, and soon we have written a whole new story, making big assumptions about the other party's thoughts and feelings.

Draw a star by the tendency above that you can relate to most.

How have you seen these concepts played out in your thought life?

I believe Joseph battled to discern through the haze of his circumstances so that he could think clearly about his dreams, his brothers, Potiphar's wife, and his plea to the cupbearer. I imagine his mind swirled with anger, fear, and thoughts of retribution such as those Louis Zamperini felt toward the Byrd.

Louis found bitterness becoming an intravenous drip of spiritual toxin that poisoned him daily. After attending a Billy Graham crusade at the urging of his wife, Louis heard the gospel and committed his life to Christ. Only through embracing Christ's forgiveness personally could he ultimately forgive the Byrd. He was able to have a letter delivered to the Byrd more than forty years after leaving prison, expressing his forgiveness and his desire that this man surrender his life to Christ. Louis had lived the torture and still cared about this man's eternity.

Forgiveness doesn't always sit well with us when it is extended toward those who have committed evil acts. We must reorient our minds to the truth that Christ died for every sinner and every sin, even the worst of offenses.

As long as Louis didn't forgive, the Byrd remained in control over him. Yet when he released the right to revenge, he found himself free. Louis went on to minister to many people with his story of grace. We, too, must be careful not to allow bitterness to grow in our relationships so that it doesn't take root and begin to consume us.

> *14 Work at living in peace with everyone, and work at living a holy life, for those who are not holy will not see the Lord. 15 Look after each other so that none of you fails to receive the grace of God. Watch out that no poisonous root of bitterness grows up to trouble you, corrupting many.*
>
> *(Hebrews 12:14-15)*

Read Hebrews 12:14-15 in the margin. What does verse 15 say a root of bitterness will do—to you and to others?

How have you seen this truth about bitterness played out in your life?

Like an acid that eats away at its container, bitterness troubles you and corrupts many. The writer of Hebrews warns us against bitterness because he knows our fleshly tendency toward it. If we aren't careful, unforgiveness won't belong to us; we will belong to it. We need God's eyes of grace in order to surrender the right to revenge and see things from His vantage point. Forgiveness frees us as much as it frees the person we are struggling to forgive. Yet as Lewis Smedes observes, "Each of us naturally puts her special spin on the inner process of forgiving the wrong. And each of us makes his own decision about how to relate to someone after we forgive her. We all play our own variations on the single forgiveness theme."[5] In order to see our situations clearly, we need a discerning mind. If we aren't careful to pursue forgiveness and clarity, we can find bitterness and a distorted view of people and situations chasing us.

As Joseph sat in his time of waiting, he had a choice about which thoughts and feelings he would dwell on and nurture. Like us, his default would be to rehearse wrongs, let bitterness grow, and allow his wounds to fester. What we naturally want to do in a relational situation is often the wrong thing. Smedes notes, "We filter the image of our villain through the gauze of our wounded memories, and in the process we alter his reality."[6]

Joseph seemed to have learned to see people through God's glasses. People are a hodgepodge of love, selfishness, kindness, fear, and the list could go on. No one is perfect. Most people aren't truly evil. They are just people who make some good decisions and some pretty bad ones. The battle for truth in relationships is often fought in our own heads and hearts. We need God's Holy Spirit desperately so that He can help us to see people clearly, soften our hearts, and revise our feelings to fall in line with His.

God longs to free us from the wasted hours of fanaticizing about our villain's demise. Joseph probably did a little bit of that. He was human. But he would have had to get off the mental hamster wheel of negative thoughts toward his brothers and his boss in order to bring his thoughts and feelings into line with God's grace. Eyes of grace come only as we surrender our thought life to God, moment by moment.

Perhaps for years some of us will regularly think of the person who wronged us. What will we do with these thoughts?

Consider the two offenses that you recorded on Day 1 (see page 43). What negative thoughts about the people who committed these offenses do you find creeping regularly into your mental routine?

What things have you tried to stop thinking about these individuals?

Tomorrow we will look more closely at how to work through fact and fiction in order to get to a place of freedom. Let's end today with a powerful weapon that God gave us to fight the battle of the mind that is especially useful in long seasons of waiting. The Apostle Paul said this in 2 Corinthians 10:5: "We demolish arguments and every pretension that sets itself up against the knowledge of God, and we take captive every thought to make it obedient to Christ" (NIV). Like Joseph, Paul served prison sentences when he was waiting to be remembered. Paul penned these words in a Roman prison. He knew what it meant to be a captive.

Prisoners don't get to do what they want to do or go where they want to go. Paul tells us to put our unforgiving thoughts into a prison cell. We are the wardens of our minds. God tells us that, with the power of the Holy Spirit, we can take thoughts captive and make them obey Christ.

Look at the following thoughts that Joseph might have had, and draw prison bars over them. (I can hear some of you who aren't visual learners groaning. If you're not up for drawing prison bars today, you can simply draw a line through each statement.)

Next, look up the Scriptures and write God's truth that counteracts these very real thoughts we sometimes cling to, especially during seasons of waiting. I've done the first one for you so that you get the idea.

If I don't pay them back for what they did, they will never learn their lesson.

(Deuteronomy 32:35)

God will take revenge.

God has forgotten about me and my dreams.

(Psalm 115:12)

I'm going to be stuck here forever.

(Jeremiah 29:11)

What about them? Why does it seem like I'm the only one with consequences in this situation?

(John 21:20-22)

Most of our mental battles come down to trust. Will we take things into our own hands, or will we apply God's truth to our very personal situations?

How about you? Which of the verses above echoes most loudly into your personal situation right now? Write this verse on an index card or in a note in your phone or tablet, and begin memorizing it. The next time your head starts spinning with thoughts focused on your own pity party, take those thoughts captive. When all you can think about is getting even or obsessing over what another person has done to you, put those thoughts in a cell and lock the door. Then repeat this verse until your thoughts and feelings come around to the side of God's truth. You'll soon notice that you are on the outside of your prison door, holding the keys to productive mental activities such as praying and encouraging others.

Oh, the hours I have wasted pursuing negative emotions. Seeing a skewed view of people and replaying old tapes of wrongs done to us steals time we could be spending listening to the voice of God for the direction we need. I have to be most on guard against these destructive thought patterns

when I'm alone in the car, waiting to pick up kids, or doing a mindless chore such as dishes or laundry. Knowing this, I try to redeem these times by listening to worship music (okay, and sometimes a little country music, too), praying, thinking of things to be thankful for, listening to sermons, or memorizing Bible verses.

Taking our thoughts captive is war, ladies! Whether we are in the thick of the battle now or enjoying an armistice in our relationships, our ability to identify and redirect our thinking will have great impact on our spiritual health. It certainly did for Joseph, setting him apart from his siblings as a leader and a man of faith.

Talk with God

Take some time now to ask the Lord to help you identify the times that you are most tempted to think negatively of others or make assumptions. Write what you hear from God in the margin.

Ask God to help you follow through in taking your thoughts captive in the midst of the daily grind as you go forward this week. Now thank God for giving you the power to take your thoughts captive and use your mind to pursue godliness and freedom. Remember 1 Corinthians 2:16: "We have the mind of Christ" (NIV).

Day 4: How Big of a Deal Is It?

As I've sat with so many women listening to their forgiveness stories, I've found that usually the ones who are willing to share are those who have gone through a significant betrayal. Each of them certainly can relate to Joseph. This week we are camped out in his prison years, asking how he stayed committed to God and others in the midst of injustice. How did he let go of the pain and learn to trust God?

Joseph also would have experienced little offenses, perhaps from other prisoners, the warden of the jail, or the cupbearer who forgot him. Today we will veer a little from the Genesis narrative to delve a little deeper into how we process offenses. While I wish we had a clearer glimpse into Joseph's heart and mind during his prison years, we do know that what happened in those years was pivotal in his journey to forgiveness.

As we learn to evaluate, pray, and search the Scriptures for wisdom about the things we don't understand in our relationships, we will find God developing our character and our trust in Him just as He did with Joseph. For starters, we need to evaluate the extent of what's been done to us. Sometimes, there is no one to forgive.

When Paula Huston published her first novel as part of a two-book contract, she received great feedback from her editor. She sacrificed a lot to get her second manuscript done while teaching at a university and parenting four children. When she submitted the second book, which wove in some religious themes after her recent return to her Christian faith, her editor rejected it and asked her to choose another topic with a more universal theme. She felt disappointed as it seemed in her mind that she was being persecuted for her faith. The editor she had once considered a friend now began to take shape as an enemy in her mind. As she took on the role of martyr, she found this thinking took on a life of its own, spilling over into her work and other areas of life. She set out to begin the process of forgiving her editor and others at the publishing house only to find there was nothing to forgive. She writes, "They'd all been acting within their understanding of what constituted integrity. They had not been 'out to get me' at all."[7]

I've found that at times I've headed down the road to bitterness, storing up what I thought were menial offenses that later became huge in my mind as I blew them out of proportion. Later I would look back on them, seeing that no wrong had actually been done. We don't need to forgive someone for moving away, not hiring us, or following God down a path that caused us some kind of loss. We forgive when someone sins against us, not when they earnestly seek the best yet their decision has negative implications for us.

As I heard my pastor husband tell the story of Mary and Martha in church recently, I heard the Holy Spirit's voice reminding me that this is a great example of a painful situation with no one to forgive. In this account, Martha is rushing around preparing food for Jesus and his entourage. Rather than enter her panic, Mary sits down at Jesus' feet to listen. Working herself into a huff (imagine her mental processes here), Martha approaches Jesus to rebuke her sister for her lack of helpfulness. Instead, Martha finds herself reprimanded. Mary has chosen the greater thing in sitting at Jesus' feet rather than worrying over details.

Ouch. That had to have stung Martha's pride. She might have inwardly been defensive or wanted to go tell a close girlfriend her side of the story so that she could be reassured and stroked. Certainly Martha did not need to forgive Jesus for what might have appeared to be insensitivity at the time. God is perfect. He never sins. Jesus spoke truth that ultimately would help Martha if she would be willing to learn from it.

This example from Scripture hits us right where it hurts, doesn't it? We can choose to be offended by things that actually are meant for our ultimate good, or we can learn from them and allow them to benefit us. A dentist drills in our mouth, and it may hurt. However, the dentist's goal is to keep us from the harm of a cavity that will cause us even more pain.

Joseph's brothers kidnapped and sold him. Potiphar's wife lied, saying Joseph attempted to rape her. Those are real offenses. We must ask God for wisdom to discover when our pain is from the difficulties of living in this world, our own ultra-sensitivity, or real wrongs perpetrated against us.

As we look at the things others have done to us, we also must consider the extent of the damage. Adam Hamilton uses the example of filling a backpack with our unforgiven blows that come in different sizes. In his book *Forgiveness: Finding Peace Through Letting Go*, he explains the difference between pebbles, medium-sized rocks, and big rocks.[8] Let me offer some ideas on each of these categories.

Pebbles

Pebbles are things such as annoyances, slights, or disappointments. We can fill a backpack full of little things and still be carrying around a lot of dead weight. Adam Hamilton names some of these pebbles, such as harsh words, an irritating glance, speeding, and little white lies.[9] When these little things are repeated over and over with wrong motives, they can become deeper and more personal wounds. Even if the hurt against us is a small thing, it can grow into a big thing if not acknowledged and forgiven.

Give an example of a smaller scale annoyance or offense:

Sometimes when we get tossed a pebble, we need to apply Colossians 3:13: "Make allowance for each other's faults, and forgive anyone who offends you. Remember, the Lord forgave you, so you must forgive others." A great example of this comes from author Leighann McCoy, who tells of a time when some of her closest friends had somehow "gotten sideways" with her pastor husband.[10] She writes,

> What I learned (the hard way) was that the more I tried to talk and reason with people, the more I created a mess. I thought that I could just proclaim truth to the women who were confused and that through my proclamation of truth I would win this thing!
>
> I underestimated the evil intent of the Enemy and overestimated my ability to talk my way out of the battle. I went over to different

people's houses and sipped coffee at their kitchen tables. I tried to love on them and reason with them and tell them all about my husband's heart. But after I went home, they took my own words, added their tainted perceptions to them, then spread them like poison all over two counties. It was as if my efforts to talk us out of trouble fueled the flames of deception!

Finally, God showed me Exodus 14:14, "The Lord will fight for you while you keep silent" (NASB).[11]

Though earlier this week we mentioned that there is a time to speak up and ask for help, sometimes God calls us to be silent while He fights our battles for us.

Can you think of a time when God led you to overlook a wrong?

Medium-Sized Rocks

Other times, medium-sized rocks are hurled in our direction. Adam Hamilton describes them as transgressions that are a little more serious, such as a hurtful comment to a husband or wife, a not-so-little lie, or dishonest gain. He writes, "Such sins, left unaddressed, especially when repeated and eventually discovered, can bring serious pain to others."[12] We often struggle to make an allowance for some of these offenses.

What steps does Matthew 18:15-17 instruct us to follow when we've been hurt? Fill in the chart below.

	Steps to Take	Positive Result	Negative Result
Step 1			Go to step 2
Step 2		Situation resolved	Go to step 3
Step 3			

When pebbles or medium-sized rocks repeatedly come our way, so much pain could be averted if we would follow God's prescriptive steps found here. All too often it seems that when we do not go to the source privately, the gossip train gets started. Even sharing with a few "safe" people is not always wise. Recently when I recounted the story of a wrong done to me to just a few close friends who do not know the other person

involved, it only seemed to fuel my fire and distort my view with each retelling. Though there is a time for speaking up and a time for seeking biblical counsel from others, that wasn't what I was doing. It was good old-fashioned venting so that I could be coddled and reassured that I was justified in my righteous anger. Usually I hear a gentle whisper or the loud alarm bells of the Holy Spirit when I trudge ahead in the flesh to speak up with wrong motives like that.

When I have prayed and talked with God about a situation first—whether I am journaling, praying silently, or talking to Him out loud—I am able to hear more clearly what my next steps should be. Sometimes He calls me to let love cover the offense, because addressing it would just blow it up bigger. Other times God reminds me of the steps in Matthew 18. If I'm still not sure what to do after diligently seeking the Lord in prayer and asking for direction, only then should I contact a trusted, godly friend who doesn't know the parties involved to ask for counsel.

> As you think about a current hurt that threatens to plant a bitter root into the soil of your life, which action is God's Spirit calling you toward? Check one of the following:
>
> __ Make an allowance for the fault.
> (Don't pick this only because you hate confrontation; if you make an allowance, then you truly must let it go with no malice.)
>
> __ Have a Matthew 18:15-17 conversation.
> (Don't pick this one only because you love to stir things up; you must follow the instructions as prescribed so that restoration can happen.)
>
> What next step should you take to put feet to this plan?

Big Rocks

There also are times when big rocks come our way. Joseph certainly had his share of them.

Being a pastor's wife for twenty years, I've heard many big rock stories, and I know that some of you reading these words have had boulders dropped on you. You have endured unspeakable cruelty at the hands of abusive parents, drunk drivers who took lives, or molesters who stole your innocence during childhood. These are just a few of the big rocks that can be dropped on us in a fallen world. Some of them can seek to crush us, leaving us with depression, anxiety, or addictions.

No allowance can be made for these offenses, and Matthew 18 might not be appropriate when you need to keep a safe distance from perpetrators. However, God can give us the power to forgive even the worst offenders so that we don't remain shackled to our abusers. Through Christ it is possible even to forgive those who have died.

Joseph became an expert in dealing with the big rocks in his life, allowing them to shape his character. Adam Hamilton writes, "We don't know how long Joseph was enslaved or in prison, but somehow during those years something happened to him. The bad things he had gone through began to shape his character in a positive way. He seemed to have been able to give his pain over to God. His soul had deepened, his dependence on God had strengthened, and his suffering had changed him from a narcissistic boy into a man of compassion and integrity."[13]

God can use your pain to shape your character as you loosen your grip and surrender it into His very capable hands. Hebrews 10:30 (NIV) reassures us that people hurling those big boulders won't walk away scot free: "For we know him who said, 'It is mine to avenge; I will repay,' and again, 'The Lord will judge his people.'" We can surrender the right to revenge and leave the execution of justice to God.

Think about any unforgiveness that might be weighing you down right now, and consider what might be filling up your backpack and straining your back. Identify below the pebbles, medium-sized rocks, and big rocks you are carrying:

Pebbles:

Medium-Sized Rocks:

Big Rocks:

God longs for you to be free. He wants to fill your thoughts with hope and peace, not bitterness and spite. Although we might like to just sing a song from the Disney movie *Frozen* and be free to "Let It Go," sometimes God calls us to take some steps in the releasing process. Ask Him to make clear what next steps you may need to take in your flight to freedom. If Joseph could forgive with God's help, I believe we can, too. Tomorrow we'll look at how this is possible, whether our backpack is full of pebbles or boulders.

Talk with God

Let's end today by praying a verse that I have clung to since I was a teenager. Over three decades ago at Falls Creek youth camp in Oklahoma, I heard God tell me that He would give me discernment if I sought Him. I began to pray this verse from the Psalms regularly, and I still whisper it often, especially when trying to make forgiveness decisions. Take a few minutes to meditate on and pray this verse to your loving God, who longs to help you discern through the haze of your pain:

> *O Lord, listen to my cry;
> give me the discerning mind you promised. (Psalm 119:169)*

Day 5: The Great Forgiver

While none of us has likely experienced cruel treatment as a prisoner of war, we have experienced deep hurts. Many of us have had some real boulders thrown our way at some point in life. For some, it hits at a very young, tender age.

My friend Trish told me about her father, who sexually and emotionally abused her as a child. She didn't tell anyone out of fear and shame, so the secret was buried inside her for many years. Mentally and emotionally, the pain was very intense and damaging. As she grew up, her dad often would comment on her body in such a negative, demeaning way that she felt ashamed of the way she looked. Later in life she became a Christ-follower, got married, and adopted children. As she experienced loving her own kids "so deeply," the question of how her father could withhold love, abuse her, and shame her in front of the family on a regular basis resurfaced.

Yesterday we sorted out the pebbles, medium-sized rocks, and big rocks of unforgiveness that weigh us down; today we ask the question, *How do we go about forgiving*? That's a critical question! How do we get past resurfacing thoughts of an abusive father without growing bitter? How do we extend grace to those who have hurt us, whether they hurled neglect, a harsh word, or a pattern of abuse our way? How did Joseph do this while waiting to be remembered in prison? Did it happen quickly or slowly over time? Did it come easier to him than it does to others?

After spending the last few months devouring many books on forgiveness as well as commentaries on Genesis, searching for as much information as possible regarding Joseph's story, I have come to believe that the answers to these questions boil down to one basic truth. Regardless of the differences in our circumstances, it is a truth that enables us to work through the pain and be free of the hangover of a wounded past.

Turn again to Matthew 18, which we looked at yesterday. Just after Jesus gives instructions about how to handle offenses, Peter asks a follow-up forgiveness question.

Read Matthew 18:21-22 and complete the following:

Peter's question: _____

Jesus' answer: _____

Some translations say seventy-seven times and others say seventy times seven. Do you think Jesus was saying we should keep track of how many times we forgive each person, so that when we get to seventy-seven or 490, we don't have to forgive anymore? Why or why not?

In family relationships alone, we could certainly go well over even 490 offenses in a lifetime; but Jesus wasn't instituting a forgiveness accounting system. In fact, he was encouraging Peter to put down the ledger sheet. To illustrate his answer, he used a story that communicates the key concept that enables us to forgive all offenses against us, whether pebbles or large stones.

Read the story in Matthew 18:23-35, and then fill in the following blanks:

The first debtor owed _____. (v. 24)

The king decided to _____. (v. 25)

Then the servant _____. (v. 26)

In response, the king relented and _____. (v. 27)

The first debtor found a fellow servant who owed him _____. (v. 28)

The fellow servant responded by _____. (v. 29)

The first debtor then decided _____. (v. 30)

When the king found out, he _____. (vv. 32-34)

First, don't miss the significant difference between the two debts. According to some translations, the first servant owed an amount of 10,000 talents. A talent was equivalent to the wages from twenty years of labor.

Most commentators agree that this would be millions of dollars in our economy. The amount is more than the servant would ever be able to repay. The second servant owed 100 denari, which is equivalent to a laborer's daily wage. Some say it would be like ten dollars in our economy, while others attribute the amount to hundreds or thousands. I guess it might depend on your current daily wage. Understanding the disparity between these two amounts provides a clearer picture of what the king in this story forgave. However, this same king also threw the unforgiving servant into prison when he refused to give grace to another man. I must admit, I've often struggled with Jesus' statement that the response of the king is what God will do to us when we don't forgive. At the end of the Lord's Prayer in Matthew 6, He makes a similar statement: "If you forgive those who sin against you, your heavenly Father will forgive you. But if you refuse to forgive others, your Father will not forgive your sins" (vv. 14-15).

God is pretty serious about forgiveness. At first glance, it seems as if forgiving others is some sort of requirement for God's forgiveness, which flies in the face of other texts indicating that salvation comes by faith alone (see Ephesians 2:8-9). Yet as I carefully read this parable in Matthew 18, I find more clarity that forgiving others isn't some sort of prerequisite to God's grace but rather a result of it. Christ is illustrating that when we withhold forgiveness from others, it reveals that perhaps we haven't fully understood and embraced the "millions" that have been forgiven us.

Forgiving others isn't some sort of requirement to get into heaven; rather, it's the outpouring of grace that overflows as we fully understand and appreciate all that God has forgiven in our lives. The more we understand God's grace toward us, the more we will, in turn, extend it to others. As I struggled through this truth in regards to my own forgiving situations—petty annoyances with loved ones, hurtful jabs from peers, or deep wounds from years past that keep resurfacing—I began to remind myself of the millions forgiven me. I would ask myself, "What's this little $10, $100, or even $1,000 situation compared to what Christ has done for me?"

Let's bring this a little closer to home. Think about yourself. In general, would you consider yourself an easily offended person?

Check the statement below that is closest to how you think others would describe you. (If you aren't sure, ask a family member or friend to pick the one that most resembles you.)

__ Most things roll off my back, and I don't take things personally very often.

__ When someone says or does something hurtful to me, I initially get pretty upset. But I try not to make assumptions about motives and give the person the benefit of the doubt.

___ Often I read things into people's facial expressions, body language, and comments that I find offensive. I don't say anything to them personally, but later I discuss it with someone who is close to me.

___ People walk on eggshells around me because they know I can be offended pretty easily, and I will let them know about it!

Social media only amplifies the opportunities to offend and be offended, because people can hide behind the screen. Sometimes we get too sensitive because of the insecurities lying beneath the surface, and sometimes people really are out to hurt us. God wants us to walk in freedom and confidence, processing our pain and moving toward forgiveness. God calls us to forgive—and perhaps, I might add, to not take things so personally all the time.

Christ modeled perfect forgiveness for us in life and in death. In Luke 23:34 we find his response to those who beat, mocked, unjustly accused, and tortured him: "Father, forgive them, for they don't know what they are doing." Imagine taking that posture in the very moment someone is hurting you. As you process the hurt in your life right now, the key to freedom from bitterness comes as you embrace God's complete forgiveness for you. This will help color how you view even those who have done evil things that have impacted your life dramatically.

Although Joseph did not know the gospel of Christ, he knew of God's desire to rescue His people through the stories of Noah, Abraham, his grandfather Isaac, and his father, Jacob. He trusted by faith in the amount of revelation that he had received. We have an even fuller understanding of God's grace and salvation. Our God sent his own Son to die on our behalf. He held nothing back to atone for our sins and erase the debt that we could never repay. He washed our sins away completely.

Look back at the pebbles, medium-sized rocks, and big rocks you identified yesterday (see page 59). Now consider each one in light of the parable we read from Matthew 18. In what ways can you relate to the unforgiving servant?

How does realizing God's grace toward you help you move toward forgiving those who have hurt you?

By understanding God's grace in her own life, my friend Trish ultimately was able to forgive her father. She's not exactly sure when the moment happened. As an adult, she confronted him, and he denied everything. Still, she was able to share that she had forgiven him, and she continues to practice forgiveness whenever a negative thought about him arises. She chooses to continually commit to forgiving him for God's glory and her own personal freedom from bitterness. Through forgivingness, she has unlocked her own prison door. You can be free, too.

In his book, *Forgive and Forget*, Lewis Smedes shares a fable about magic eyes. These are eyes that look for the best in others and seek to forgive, rather than hold on to the offenses of others with self-righteous judgment. These magic eyes develop the more we are aware of our own failures and God's amazing grace toward us.[14]

As we end today, take a few minutes to reflect on the ways you have needed God's grace this week.

List three things God has forgiven you for this week:

1.

2.

3.

Whether your list includes sinful thoughts, attitudes, or actions, the truth is that we all struggle against our flesh and sometimes make mistakes. The good news is that God doesn't keep any lists like this. He forgives freely and chooses not to remember all the mistakes we have made. While God isn't forgetful, He intentionally chooses as an act of His will not to remember all the bad things we've done: "And I will forgive their wickedness, / and I will never again remember their sins" (Hebrews 8:12).

Go ahead and cross out all three items on your list above. You can even use a marker so that they are completely blotted out.

We probably won't forget the wrongs committed against us. However, like our loving Father, we can choose as an act of our wills not to remember them—not to dwell on them. By focusing on truth and gaining perspective on the offenses of others in light of the offenses God has forgiven us, we can forgive as we've been forgiven.

Talk with God

Meditate on truth about how God sees you. Relish God's amazing grace to forgive you—a million times over. He is relentless in loving you, and He wants to equip you with His supernatural power to forgive others. Pray the following verses to Him, thanking Him for what He has done and continues to do in forgiving you.

> *¹⁰ He does not punish us for all our sins;*
> *   he does not deal harshly with us, as we deserve.*
> *¹¹ For his unfailing love toward those who fear him*
> *   is as great as the height of the heavens above the earth.*
> *¹² He has removed our sins as far from us*
> *   as the east is from the west.*
> *¹³ The LORD is like a father to his children,*
> *   tender and compassionate to those who fear him.*
> *¹⁴ For he knows how weak we are;*
> *   he remembers we are only dust. (Psalm 103:10-14)*

> *"I—yes, I alone—will blot out your sins for my own sake and will never think of them again." (Isaiah 43:25)*

> *He is so rich in kindness and grace that he purchased our freedom with the blood of his Son and forgave our sins.*
> *   (Ephesians 1:7)*

Look for truths about God's forgiveness in these verses, and thank Him for them. Then write one or two key words below that you can use to remind yourself of these truths the next time you want to shake down someone for the debt you feel he or she owes you. Meditate on these key words, write them on index cards, or make a note in your phone or tablet. You never know how soon you may need them so that you won't act the part of the unforgiving servant in your next forgiveness story!

Digging Deeper

Joseph had dreams, and two of his inmates received messages from God in dreams. What was the significance of biblical dreams? Does God still communicate with us in this way? Find out in the online Digging Deeper article for Week 2, "Dreams and Dreamers" (see AbingdonPress.com/Joseph).

Waiting to Be Remembered

The _____ glasses:
When we are new in a relationship or situation; when everything looks good.

The glasses of _____:
When we look at people through a dark lens.

Then he sent someone to Egypt ahead of them—
Joseph, who was sold as a slave.
They bruised his feet with fetters
and placed his neck in an iron collar.
Until the time came to fulfill his dreams,
the LORD tested Joseph's character. (Psalm 105:17-19)

You keep track of all my sorrows.

You have collected all my _____ in your bottle.
You have recorded each one in your book. (Psalm 56:8)

"And please remember me and do me a favor when things go well for you. Mention me to Pharaoh, so he might let me out of this place. For I was kidnapped from my homeland, the land of the Hebrews, and now I'm here in prison, but I did nothing to deserve it." (Genesis 40:14-15)

3 Temptations When We Are Hurt:

1. We have a tendency to believe that if we forgive someone, it will minimize or

   _____ what they did.

2. We judge other people by their _____, but we judge ourselves by

   our _____.

3. We grow _____ in our head. (We make assumptions.)

VIDEO VIEWER GUIDE: WEEK 2

The _____ glasses:
When our unforgiveness no longer belongs to us; we belong to it.

If anyone claims, "I am living in the light," but hates a fellow believer, that person is still living in darkness. Anyone who loves a fellow believer is living in the light and does not cause others to stumble. But anyone who hates a fellow believer is still living and walking in darkness. Such a person does not know the way to go, having been blinded by the darkness. (1 John 2:9-11)

Unforgiveness is one of the biggest ways that we can become _____.

The _____ glasses:
When we can see clearly with a heart of love.

God's _____ are not always His _____.

Then Pharaoh sent for him and set him free;
        the ruler of the nation opened his prison door.
Joseph was put in charge of all the king's household;
        he became ruler over all the king's possessions.
He could instruct the king's aides as he pleased
        and teach the king's advisers. (Psalm 105:20-22)

Matthew 18:21-35 – The Parable of the Unforgiving Servant

He has _____ our sins as far from us

        as the east is from the west. (Psalm 103:12)

Week 3

DREAMS COMING TRUE

Genesis 41–42

Memory Verse

"So, my dear brothers and sisters, be strong and immovable. Always work enthusiastically for the Lord, for you know that nothing you do for the Lord is ever useless."

(1 Corinthians 15:58)

Day 1: The Second Story

My sister has been living in limbo for quite a few years. Her husband's job hasn't seemed like the right fit for a long time. The family spent one summer away from their home in New Jersey to pray and seek God's wisdom, but no clear direction came. Her husband interviewed for jobs in several different states, but no doors were swinging open. This went on for months and then years, and their spirits deflated over and over again as nothing seemed to be changing. They felt cornered in a place called "in between." It was difficult to make decisions about kids' activities, schools, and church commitments, knowing that they probably would be leaving the state. She wondered if it was wise to keep investing in relationships with friends, which would only intensify the pain of goodbyes that might come in the near future. Why did they have such a discontent coupled with no clear leads for a change? Had God forgotten them? It sure felt that way for a time.

Joseph also spent a long time in an in-between place. Even while in prison, he held to his clear dreams of leadership and authority, which bore no resemblance to the landscape of servitude where he found himself living. Had God forgotten him? Some days it might have seemed that way as he wore shackles on his feet and an iron collar around his neck.

Joseph believed that God was working out His invisible plans even during dark days. Though he lived on the "bottom floor" of prison, somehow he trusted that there was a "second story"—an upper level where God was doing a work. Joseph couldn't understand it, but he chose to believe there was a greater plan. Warren Wiersbe writes, "Joseph had time to think and pray and to ponder the meaning of the two dreams God had sent him. He would learn that God's delays are not God's denials."[2]

Read Genesis 41:1-15 and answer the following questions:

How many years have passed since Joseph asked the cupbearer to remember him? (v. 1)

Fun Fact:

"The Egypt in which Joseph found himself was primarily a land of small villages inhabited by peasants who worked the land and raised grain and vegetables."[1]

What caused the cupbearer to remember Joseph? (vv. 8-9)

How did Pharaoh respond when the cupbearer explained what Joseph had done in prison? (v. 14)

Here we get a glimpse into Joseph's rise from the dungeon. We see Wiersbe's words coming true for Joseph: God's delays are not God's denials. God gave Joseph dreams of ruling, and Joseph held on to those dreams even at his lowest point. He believed that the day would arrive when his dreams would come true, and here in Chapter 41 we see the tide beginning to turn. Joseph begins to move from his in-between waiting time toward the fulfillment of his dreams.

Have you ever experienced firsthand that God's delays are not His denials? Can you think of a time when you thought something would never happen, and then it did? Write about it below:

While God's timing doesn't always line up with what makes most sense to us, He is certainly never late. We see another powerful truth in this passage as Joseph's position is elevated by the leader of all of Egypt: *One small decision can change the course of your future.*

After the cupbearer and the baker were sent to prison, the captain of the guard assigned them to Joseph's care. One day Joseph noticed that they were dejected. When he inquired about their sadness, they mentioned that they both had experienced vivid dreams. Joseph knew about dreams. His dreams had so angered his brothers that their response had started a chain reaction of events that had put him in this prison.

When I remember that Joseph's dreams were of his brothers' sheaves of grain bowing down to his, and of him ruling over the sun and moon and eleven stars, it's a wonder to me that Joseph maintained such a high view of God even when these dreams were indefinitely delayed. If I put myself in his shoes—in prison, suffering unjustly—I might have responded to the cupbearer's and baker's dreams like this: "I wouldn't put too much stock in those dreams. I had one about ruling, and look at me now. If I were you, I would try as hard as possible to forget those nightmares."

Joseph didn't perpetuate a pity party as I sometimes have done over much less important things. He had faith that God was still going to fulfill His promises to elevate him. He knew there was a second story where God was at work. By deciding to interpret the two servants' dreams and

ask the cupbearer for help, he later found that they became the linchpin that knocked down his prison walls. Joseph's small decision to discern the meaning of their dreams—both of which came to pass just as he had said—ultimately landed him a whole new position, as we will see later this week.

As we've noted, two years went by before the cupbearer remembered Joseph—two long years before his circumstances budged at all. Yet serious dream fulfillment eventually would follow this seemingly forgotten kindness to a servant.

In my own life, I often find God working in the "smalls"—those decisions when no one is looking; that risk you take because God's Holy Spirit keeps nagging you to step out in faith; a friend you invite over who later becomes a lifelong kindred spirit. Our obedience in the smalls echoes big into the future. God calls us to be faithful in all things, believing in His goodness in the midst of bad circumstances.

Even if you are choosing what tone to use, deciding where your thoughts dwell, or calling a friend, one of those small decisions might echo big into your future. Every choice we make today will have an impact for God's kingdom. Whether we're at work with projects to complete or at home with a laundry basket in front of us, what we decide matters. Our choices in attitudes, words, and actions set the tone in our environment.

My sister has had plenty of opportunities to be faithful in the smalls of life during a long season of waiting. She and her husband ended up making a cross-country move with their three children without having jobs or a home. Though they both now have jobs, everything didn't turn out as they had expected. The challenges of adjusting to different schools, jobs, and people have caused them to cling to Christ and one another. As a result, my sister would say that her marriage and faith have grown stronger and their children have the benefit of living nearer to cousins and extended family. God never left them, although for a time they couldn't see His work. Even now everything doesn't make sense, but they believe that God will bring good from the pain. Like Joseph, they are coming out of the dark, and they can see that God has been building a second story in their lives. They know that their faithfulness during this time has not been useless.

Read 1 Corinthians 15:58 in the margin. How did this verse prove true in Joseph's life regarding his choice to interpret the dreams of some prison inmates?

So, my dear brothers and sisters, be strong and immovable. Always work enthusiastically for the Lord, for you know that nothing you do for the Lord is ever useless.

(1 Corinthians 15:58)

Initially Joseph's interpretation of the cupbearer's dream seemed like an opportunity for justice, and later it appeared to be a complete dead end. But we know from 1 Corinthians 15:58 that if we do something enthusiastically for God—not to please people—it is *never* useless. Joseph would soon reap the truth of this verse. Whether or not we understand the purpose of something, God will use it in the second story He is working to complete in our lives.

Let's look at our lives as a two-story house. Both floors work together to make up the home. The first floor is where we currently live—it's the nuts and bolts of daily life—the joys, the challenges, and at times, the monotony. This is the stuff we are doing, seeing, feeling, and thinking about in the daily grind. The second floor is where God is building character and using our lives to carry out His purposes. Upstairs God is bringing benefit out of even the worst situations we face on the ground level.

Perhaps an example of Joseph's two-story house will help us as we move through this exercise. First, I've written some statements describing Joseph's possible first floor life.

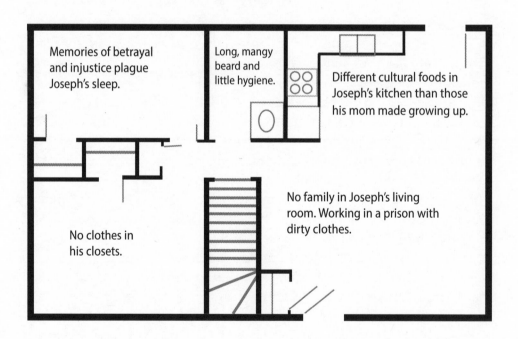

Now it's your turn. If your life were divided up into rooms, what would your first floor look like right now? Are there diapers to change or toys to pick up in the bedroom? A car leaving your garage for work? Lots of kitchen activity? I often think of a bedroom in our house that is empty as our oldest has left for college.

Label the first floor of your home with your daily stuff of life.

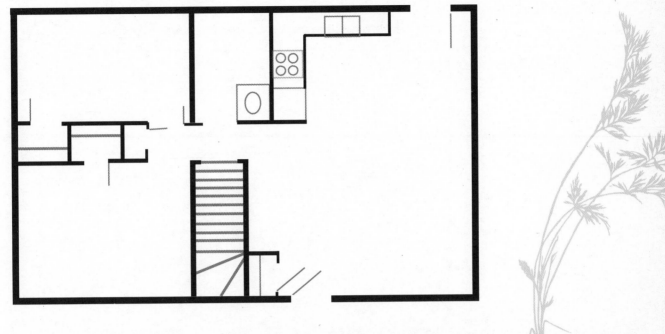

Now let's consider the second story of Joseph's house. Without knowing the mind of God but having the benefit of hindsight, let's look at what could have been happening on Joseph's second floor. Again, this is the work that God was doing through Joseph's difficult circumstances.

While in the midst of it Joseph couldn't always see and appreciate how God was using his trials and joys to work out a plan, he trusted that there was a second story being built. Even when we can't identify how and why God is allowing things in our lives, we, too, can trust that something is happening upstairs.

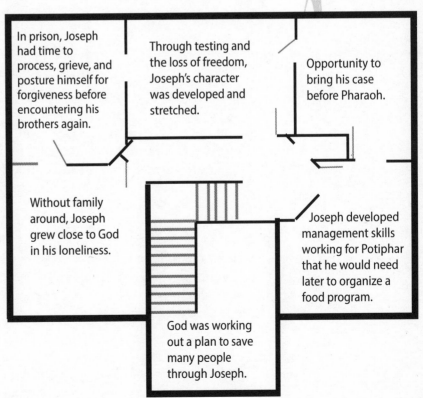

In prison, Joseph had time to process, grieve, and posture himself for forgiveness before encountering his brothers again.

Through testing and the loss of freedom, Joseph's character was developed and stretched.

Opportunity to bring his case before Pharaoh.

Without family around, Joseph grew close to God in his loneliness.

Joseph developed management skills working for Potiphar that he would need later to organize a food program.

God was working out a plan to save many people through Joseph.

As you reflect on your life, are there circumstances, events, or challenges that you couldn't understand at the time but now see how God used them for His greater work? If so, write them in the second-story floor plan below:

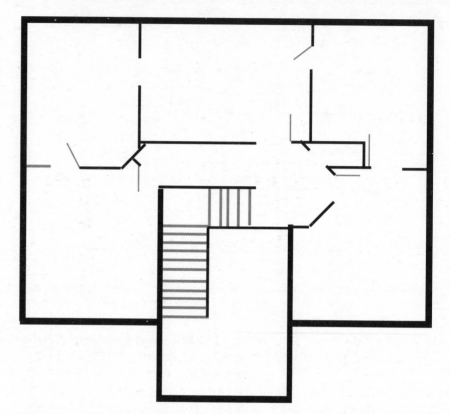

While certainly no one knows the mind of God (1 Corinthians 2:16), I do believe it can be helpful to look for ways God might be working. We can ask questions such as these: What might the Lord be doing on my second story? Is He preparing me for something? How could He use these first-floor circumstances to be growing my faith? I know that in my own life, God has used trials to prepare me, introduce me to people, and help me grow in faith and dependence.

Joseph couldn't have realized how his time serving Potiphar or his jail sentence would lead him to the fulfillment of his dreams. However, he exercised faith to believe God even when he couldn't see. Like Joseph, you can begin to see a second story. Don't quit trusting and believing that God will fulfill His promises to you. Remember, His delays are not His denials; one small decision can change the course of your future.

Talk with God

Spend some time asking God to help you begin to see your struggles with a new perspective as you trust that He is working on a second story in your life. Ask Him to give you a glimpse into what He is doing, and write any ideas in the margin. Tell Him you are willing to trust Him through the in-between times of your life.

Day 2: Humble and Bold

As I sat at a breakfast table with a group of about ten women on my first day in Kenya, I waited anxiously to talk with Pamela. I knew this pastor's wife only from a book I had read about her family. *Bernard's Vision* tells the story of a pastor in Kenya who left his wife and their four small children in the care of other local pastors in order to further his Bible education in the United States. But things didn't turn out as planned. Pamela didn't get the expected help and was turned out on the street by her landlord. God cared for them even as they squatted in a room in a slum, searching for daily food. When word reached her husband of his family's plight, he told his story to those at the school he was attending and was able to get a job cleaning the library. This provided enough money for Pamela to begin renting a small piece of land where she could grow things to sell. She also sewed and sold dresses to feed her family.

I was struck not only by this young family's faith and determination, but also by their ability to forgive. For decades they would work with these same pastors who had promised to help but didn't follow through. The book mentioned that Pamela's husband had a harder time forgiving than she did. I wanted to know *how*—how did she ever get over it? When I put myself in her shoes, I wondered if I ever would.

So I asked her. I looked into her eyes shining with the joy of Jesus and told her I had read her story. I asked her simply, "Pamela, how did you forgive the people responsible for putting you and your children on the street?" She answered with humility as well as boldness. She said that God had forgiven all of her sin on the cross, and that He commanded her to forgive. Her own humble dependence on God, coupled with her strong belief that anything is possible with God, helped her forgive those whose decisions had brought drastic consequences in her family's life.

Like Joseph, Pamela had experienced real hunger and heartache at the expense of others.

Turn to Genesis 41 and look again at verses 14-15 that we read yesterday. Where did Joseph come from on this day?

Who is he now standing in front of?

We see Joseph moving on up! Let's pick up the story where we left off.

Read Genesis 41:16, and write Joseph's response to Pharaoh in your own words below:

Joseph notes an important spiritual truth in this verse: "It is beyond my power to do this." Though Joseph had been an imprisoned slave, now he was standing before the highest authority in Egypt with an incredible opportunity before him. And what did he do? He acknowledged that he was unable to help in his own power. One commentary offers this observation: "It is not often that men and women in high places admit that they are not capable of coping and that they need genuine spirituality to enable them to lead and guide their fellow men in God's world."[3]

Pharaoh faced a puzzling circumstance. Egypt's highest ruler was typically protected from bad news. With his god-like status, he wasn't to be bothered with problems. When Pharaoh issued a command, those serving under him were to make it happen without bringing difficulties to him. Pharaoh had no practice with dealing with bad news, but as one source notes, "The dream penetrates the royal isolation."[4] He couldn't sleep because of these dreams that made no sense to him. His magicians and wise men couldn't seem to help him out. After the cupbearer told him about Joseph, he hoped that this young Hebrew would be able to provide some clarity.

Like Pharaoh, we also look for answers. Though dreams about cows and grain may not be interrupting our sleep, many of us lie awake with all sorts of puzzling thoughts. We wonder

- how to pay our bills at the end of the month.
- what to do about a project at work that we don't feel qualified to execute.
- where to turn for help with a marriage that lost its spark years ago and now feels like a trap.
- how to forgive the friend who wounded us so deeply with her words and actions.
- if our child will ever recover from this physical and emotional struggle.

What keeps you awake at night may not be one of these scenarios, but chances are some situation crosses your mind continually before you fall asleep. Does anything come to mind right now? It may not be your own problem. As with Joseph, another person may be looking to you for a solution. Perhaps a boss, family member, or friend has come to you in hopes that you can provide a fix to help *them* sleep better at night.

Describe what is on your mind these days, whether it is your own problem or someone else's:

No matter which situation you find yourself in, the answer remains the same. It is beyond our power to make it all right. Joseph understood the truth of John 15:5 long before it was penned.

Read John 15:5 in the margin and fill in the blank:

"Apart from me, you can do _____."

We need to stop trying to fix our own problems or those of others around us. Like Joseph, we must start by admitting that we can't do it on our own. We need God's help. The posture of humility displayed in this scene before Pharaoh's throne echoes with relevancy into so many facets of life.

God doesn't leave us in a state of helplessness when we realize we can't solve our problems on our own. He wants to provide insight and set our minds at ease. He doesn't want us to continue in sleepless agony over things we can't understand, much less change. We can say along with Joseph, "It is beyond my power to do this....But God..." (Genesis 41:16). Those last two words change everything.

Complete the statements below in regard to a situation you are currently facing:

It is beyond my power to _____.

But God _____.

Pharaoh recounts his dreams to Joseph in Genesis 41:17-24. Then Joseph interprets them in verses 25-36.

Read Genesis 41:17-24 and briefly summarize Pharaoh's two dreams below:

Dream 1:

Dream 2:

Now read Joseph's interpretations in Genesis 41:25-36. Summarize the meaning of the dreams by writing what each picture represents:

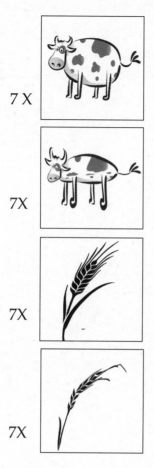

7 X

7X

7X

7X

According to verse 32, why did Pharaoh have the dream twice?

What do you notice about Joseph's demeanor and tone as he explains the dreams? Circle words below that best describe his delivery:

Scared   Unsure   Bold   Timid

Confident   Fearful   Respectful   Solution-oriented

This passage does not evoke a picture of Joseph shuffling his feet and looking at the floor like a foreign prisoner. We see a bold Joseph who is sure of himself, commanding the room. His confidence is not in himself but in the God who has helped him take steps toward forgiveness in a dungeon for the last few years.

Look back through verses 16-32 and note every time Joseph mentions God:

Verse number	What Joseph says about God
16	
25	
28	
32	

Joseph credited the God of heaven as the interpreter of dreams. He said confidently that God would answer his question about Pharaoh's dream. Joseph's words are not eloquent or impressive, but his ability to elevate God in his explanation with great humility and boldness is extraordinary. Joseph's faith seemed as sure as his new clothes and freshly shaven face. Joseph saw firsthand that although his dreams had been a long time in the making, they would not be denied forever. God was working out His plan on His own timetable. For Joseph, this meant that his prison term was coming to an end. In your life as well, the time of waiting will not last forever.

Pamela eventually got out of the slums and moved her family back into a home with her husband. They began an orphan home and medical center, and they began working with their church to reach people for Christ. Along with her husband, she especially has a heart for children on the streets in Kenya who are in danger of becoming addicted to huffing glue.

When Pamela came out of her difficult time, she had to make a decision about forgiveness. She realized it was more than she could do on her own. Although it was not in her power to forgive, she believed wholeheartedly that God would enable her to do it through His strength.

Like Pamela, we can humbly admit that we need help in extending grace to others and then confidently forgive them, believing that God will supply all we need to see it through.

Talk with God

When you feel overwhelmed with the need to forgive or by some other situation that is keeping you awake at night, remember Joseph's example. He humbly admitted that dream interpretation was beyond him. Take a minute right now and make a similar statement to God:

God, I can't figure out _____ on my own anymore. It is not in my power to do it.

Coupled with Joseph's humility was his boldness. He believed His God could do anything. Finish your prayer in this way:

God, I boldly proclaim that You have got this situation. Please put my mind at ease and show me what You are calling me to do next. Amen.

You might be tempted to take back what you just released to God. I have a feeling that Joseph regularly practiced surrender. It wasn't just a one-time thing. So next time sleep won't come, remember to practice the humility and boldness of Joseph, and you just might find a new direction for the future taking shape in your life.

Day 3: From Zero to Hero

Now we've reached the point in the story where the tide really begins to turn for Joseph. He will go from serving inmates and cleaning out prison cells to a place of great power and authority.

Read Genesis 41:37-57 and draw a line to connect each reference with the new thing(s) that happened for Joseph.

command of Pharaoh's court	verse 45
fine clothing	verses 50-52
new name, wife	verses 40-41
two sons	verse 42

We also find in verses 56-57 that Joseph had a great new purpose in providing for many lives during the famine. Put yourself in Joseph's shoes. How do you think it must have felt to finally have all of these blessings?

We get a glimpse into Joseph's heart through the naming of his children. Look at verses 50-52 and write below the meanings of his two sons' names:

Manasseh: _____

Ephraim: _____

If ever we are tempted to think Joseph didn't struggle to forgive the pain from his past, we can dispel that myth here. Manasseh's name proves that he had struggled to forget the wounds his brothers inflicted many years ago. During the waiting time he processed and prayed, but now God's blessings serve as a balm to propel him into deeper healing.

What are some blessings God has provided in your life recently? Try to name at least three:

1.

2.

3.

How might seeing these blessings as God's provision given to help you overcome and forget some of the pain from your past move you into deeper healing?

Joseph now holds a great position of authority. I can imagine his joy at simple pleasures that had been denied him for so long. He could walk around freely, take baths, eat good food, and enjoy his wife and children. Family had been something stolen from him long ago. Now he has a family of his own. His circumstances remind me of the fictional character in *The Count of Monte Cristo* named Edmond. Much like Joseph, Edmond's best friend betrays him, and he ends up unjustly sentenced to endure a horrible life in prison. There he meets a priest who tries to teach him about forgiveness and moving forward. However, Edmond's pain festers and grows into bitterness coupled with a strong desire for revenge. Edmond escapes and finds the treasure of Sparta, which brings him wealth and power. When he goes from zero to hero, he uses his power in an attempt to exact revenge on those responsible for his years of suffering. Ultimately he surrenders to the priest's wisdom, finding no peace in his quest. Instead, he spends his energy pursuing love and family rather than vengeance.

As second in command, Joseph would have the power to get back at Potiphar, Potiphar's wife, and even the cupbearer for forgetting him for two long years. But this isn't what we read in the text. Instead we find Joseph celebrating his new blessings and working hard to oversee a divine plan to save people from famine.

As I think about my own life, there have been times when I have been guilty of allowing one small negative thought to ruin my ability to see the many blessings around me. Can you relate? As you think about

Fun Fact:
Pharaoh's dreams mentioned the number seven many times. Seven—sometimes called the number of perfection or completion—is a significant number in the Bible. Just a few mentions of the number seven include the number of creation days, the number of times Joshua marched around Jericho, and the number of churches, stars, and lampstands in the Book of Revelation.

the blessings you listed earlier, can you think of something that might be hindering you from fully appreciating them? It might be a grudge against a friend or family member that just keeps spoiling your ability to enjoy life. A difficult marriage might overshadow blessings of children and friendships. Perhaps you are reading meaning into the words from a text or social media comment, and your overanalytical brain won't stop making assumptions. Whatever it may be, we can learn from Joseph's example of appreciation and productivity.

What task has God put in front of you that could shift your focus from negative thoughts to productive energy?

As you shift from dwelling on the past to focusing on this task from God, you can gain some ground toward forgiveness and the ability to more fully enjoy your blessings.

Joseph was in uncharted territory regarding the task of reaping extra food and storing it. This wasn't a common practice because famine was rare in Egypt. One source notes, "Times of great plenty were nothing new to the land of Egypt but times of extended famine were most unusual because the ecology of the land was related to the Nile which was most consistent in its supply."[5]

Though Pharaoh experienced the dreams firsthand and believed Joseph's interpretation, I'm sure there were others who didn't agree with Joseph's proposal or placement as ruler and who challenged his plans to store so much extra food. Still, Joseph pressed on to organize, store, and prepare for years of famine ahead. Although he knew the plan to be divine, he was called to put feet to that plan. Joseph played an important role in carrying out God's plan. One commentator writes this:

> The firm purpose of God requires bold royal action. The intervention of God does not end royal responsibility, but sets it in a context where a new course of action is required. God's purpose is not the end of human planning but the ground for it. That God's "plan" is above human "plans" ... does not mean there should not be human planning. It means that it must be responsive and faithful to God's plan.[6]

In other words, we are active participants in God's divine plan!

Like Joseph, we have a role to play in God's divine plan. God wants each of us to set our mind to prepare and do the work He has put before us. Whether our work is feeding babies, managing employees, teaching students, or something else, God calls us to do it with all our heart. When we sit and stew over personal injustices, we waste time and energy that could be spent in greater productivity. As Joseph was elevated from zero to hero, he used his new freedoms and resources to help others. You might say that he passed the power test.

Many great biblical characters went through a time of difficulty as they learned to rely on God. David lived in caves. Daniel endured captivity in a foreign land. However, their later tests of prosperity and power also helped to prove their character. David struggled and learned through his abuse of power in taking another man's wife. Daniel passed the test of prosperity by continuing to pray even when under pressure.

It's tempting to want to stick it to the people who've hurt you when it's in your power to do so. Yet Joseph kept his attention on the task at hand and left vengeance to God.

Read Leviticus 19:18 in the margin. What is the first command given in this verse?

> *"Do not seek revenge or bear a grudge against anyone among your people, but love your neighbor as yourself. I am the LORD."*
>
> *(Leviticus 19:18 NIV)*

What is the second instruction?

Joseph lived these words. He spent his energy loving his neighbors by interpreting Pharaoh's dream and then making careful preparation for the years of famine ahead.

Are there any grudges you need to offer up to God right now?

In what ways can you put your energy into "loving your neighbor" today?

As we allow God to guide us on our personal journeys to forgiveness, we will find our focus shifting from inward processing to outward ministry. Though we are always working through issues, we can expend less mental energy on making assumptions and worrying and more time on loving and serving others. Our loving God knows that working hard and helping others is healing for our own souls.

Talk with God

Whether you feel that you are in the "zero" phase of waiting to be remembered or the "hero" season when blessings seem to abound, God calls you to be faithful. Spend some time praising Him right now for the blessings in your life and the work He has set before you. Joseph served others as a prisoner and as a leader. He was faithful with a little and then entrusted with much more. Ask God to show you how you might love and serve those around you today. Then take some time to quietly listen for His voice. Record in the margin any thoughts He brings to mind.

End your prayer time meditating on this verse from Matthew 25:23:

The master said, "Well done, my good and faithful servant. You have been faithful in handling this small amount, so now I will give you many more responsibilities. Let's celebrate together!"

Day 4: Responders and Reactors

Not long ago my friend Carla reacted when she wishes she had responded. She received a message from someone whose daughter recently had been over for a playdate with Carla's daughter and had seen a picture of some mutual friends on a bulletin board with their eyes blacked out with a marker. After receiving the message, Carla rushed to find the photo on the bulletin board in the kitchen, which was crowded with Christmas card pictures and baby announcements from family and friends. She didn't remember receiving a picture of this particular family, and with a hurried glance she missed seeing the small wallet-sized family photo. The Holy Spirit cautioned her as her fingers flew to the phone to text back a retort that no such picture existed. She didn't heed His voice and justified her quick reaction and defensiveness.

How she wishes she had waited. In time it came to light that the words in the voicemail were true. Though her daughter hadn't purposely been hurtful, she had in fact doodled on the photo, coloring in the eyes with a marker. Oh, how the enemy got some mileage out of it, and she only inflamed the situation by reacting—defensively and emotionally. Later she called to apologize, but damage had been done to an already fragile relationship. They had been moving forward, and Carla's poor reaction sent them back quite a few steps.

In today's world of social media and instant communication, we need even greater restraint when faced with situations that tempt us to react. Whether we are coming face-to-face with those who have hurt us or

answering when an offense is brought against us, the inclination to say or do something immediately can be overwhelming. I know I am especially sensitive to this when others criticize my children. I've also witnessed some great friendships torn apart over skirmishes between children, extended family members, or mutual friends. We need time to see things clearly so that we don't act first and think later.

Every human on the planet struggles to patiently respond instead of emotionally react. We find Joseph having a very emotional day in this next part of his story. In Genesis 42 we find his face-to-face encounter with his brothers.

Read Genesis 42:1-20. Why do the brothers travel to Egypt?

Fun Fact:

"The trip to Egypt was long (250–300 miles) and dangerous, and a round trip could consume six weeks' time."[7]

One commentator observes, "While he [Joseph] was busy putting his nationwide disaster intervention plan into action, his brothers and father were beginning to feel the pinch of famine in their bellies."[8] Joseph knew the famine spread far and wide. God had said that it would. Joseph already might have sold grain to others from regions near Canaan where his family lived. Perhaps he was anticipating the arrival of his brothers, or maybe he was so caught up in his work that they had drifted to a back corner of his mind.

In either case, the old forgiveness issue was now up front and personal. It was right in front of him. Can you relate with Joseph's predicament? Out of nowhere you see those who have hurt you. You are going about your business, and something from your past resurfaces.

Can you recall a time in your life when you found yourself face-to-face with a person who had hurt you in the past? If so, what were some of the emotions you experienced?

Did you react, respond, or avoid the situation?

I know my own tendency is to react or avoid. While we can't get inside Joseph's head, let's think through his behavior in this text. Specifically, let's look at Joseph's posture here so that we can see a change later in the text after he has had time for prayer and consideration.

Read Genesis 42:6-12 below, which describes Joseph's initial interaction with his brothers. Circle any words or phrases that give us clues about Joseph's emotional demeanor, labeling them with a "J." Circle words that describe his brothers' emotional posture, labeling them with a "B." I have done two for you as examples.

B — *⁶ Since Joseph was governor of all Egypt and in charge of selling grain to all the people, it was to him that his brothers came. When they arrived, they (bowed) before him with their faces to the ground. ⁷ Joseph recognized his brothers instantly, but he pretended to be a stranger and spoke (harshly)*

J — *to them. "Where are you from?" he demanded.*

"From the land of Canaan," they replied. "We have come to buy food."

⁸ Although Joseph recognized his brothers, they didn't recognize him. ⁹ And he remembered the dreams he'd had about them many years before. He said to them, "You are spies! You have come to see how vulnerable our land has become."

¹⁰ "No, my lord!" they exclaimed. "Your servants have simply come to buy food. ¹¹ We are all brothers—members of the same family. We are honest men, sir! We are not spies!"

¹² "Yes, you are!" Joseph insisted. "You have come to see how vulnerable our land has become." (Genesis 42:6-12)

Sum up in one sentence how Joseph seems to react:

What impression do you get of Joseph's brothers from these verses?

Scholars have many opinions about why Joseph reacted this way, including the following:

1. He might have been acting the part of a strong Egyptian leader who had concerns that others were watching.
2. Perhaps he had planned all along to react this way in an attempt to keep his brothers in town by calling them spies.
3. Another possibility is that he was caught off guard and made something up on the spot to buy him some more time to figure out his next step.

4. Another idea is that Joseph's intent was to bait his brothers into bringing Benjamin and his father back to him.

As you think about how you have felt when you have been caught off guard by a face-to-face encounter with someone who caused you pain, which of the responses above would you postulate were Joseph's possible motives in this situation? Write the number or numbers below and why you picked each:

Do you have other ideas about what his motives might have been? If so, describe them below:

Of course, we will never know for sure what Joseph's motives were, but we can gain insight from his next move.

Read verse 17 in the margin. What did Joseph do next?

> *So Joseph put them all in prison for three days.*
>
> *(Genesis 42:17)*

As I have studied and learned about Joseph's character and strategy throughout these last chapters of Genesis, I have come to believe that even this initial reaction could have been a plan for ultimate reconciliation rather than immediate retribution. Not knowing exactly what was going on inside his heart and mind, I do see a valuable lesson here for us that I call the rule of response. It involves waiting so that painful emotions can get "shaken out" like a dirty rug. When something gets stirred inside of us that evokes either new or old feelings of pain, we would do well to take a pause before making any decisions we might regret.

How many times has something made you mad and you have had your fingers on the keyboard of an electronic device, wanting to react rather than respond? We would do well to delete that passive-aggressive social media post that we know is aimed at only a few people, that e-mail with a few choice words that has thrown us into a typing frenzy of justification, or that text we aren't sure how to take since it has no smiley emoticon. Rather than reacting immediately, we need time to reflect, pray, and ask God for wisdom.

Joseph took three days for his rule of response. In our fast-paced world, you might not have three full days to respond; but at least try to follow the twenty-four-hour rule. Whatever it is that you want to react to—big or small—just wait. Think. Pray. Ask God for wisdom. Allow time for your emotions to settle so that you can see things more clearly.

Read Genesis 42:18-20 in the margin. What changes do you notice in Joseph since his original display at the grain counter?

Here we find Joseph much more in control of his emotions and with a confident plan. He overhears his brothers talking in verses 21 and 22:

> ²¹ *"Clearly we are being punished because of what we did to Joseph long ago. We saw his anguish when he pleaded for his life, but we wouldn't listen. That's why we're in this trouble."*
> ²² *"Didn't I tell you not to sin against the boy?" Reuben asked. "But you wouldn't listen. And now we have to answer for his blood!*

We find a detail here that we only surmised earlier in the story. Joseph was terrified and pleading in that hole over a decade ago as a teenage boy. Hearing his brothers talk of it might have taken him right back to that place even now as a husband and father in his thirties. It seemed to reopen an old wound. He named his first child Manasseh, meaning that now he could forget; but in this moment the old pain comes up fresh and he can't keep his feelings from spilling over.

What does he do next according to verse 24?

Have you ever had a time when an old wound resurfaced and you were overcome with emotion?

I find that it's especially difficult to hear someone else tell your story from his or her point of view when you are the one who has lived the hurt, the struggle to forgive, and the consequences of the other person's decisions. No two people remember the same event the same way. Proverbs 14:10 says, "Each heart knows its own bitterness, / and no one else can fully share its joy."

Joseph's brothers could not have appreciated his pain, the separation from his father, and the prison sentence he had endured as a result of their betrayal. Now he had been exalted, and his dreams had come full circle. His brothers bowed before him, and he held their future in his hands. Again Joseph did what he had done before—he took a break so that he could gather himself and reenter the dialogue.

Joseph's brothers spoke of what they did to Joseph only in terms of God punishing them for it. We don't hear great remorse over what their brother might have endured in captivity. Instead they were concerned about their own consequences for their actions. Joseph needed time to sort through his perception of what his brothers said, what had happened as a result, and what God intended to do through it all.

Perception and truth don't always line up exactly. How we perceive a look, a comment, or an action isn't always congruent with the originator's intent. We tend to judge others by their actions, but we judge ourselves by our intentions. Like Joseph, we also need time to sort through our feelings and thoughts when we interact with people with whom we have complicated relationships.

> *We tend to judge others by their actions, but we judge ourselves by our intentions.*

Can you think of and describe a time when you wrongly made an assumption about someone else's motives?

How do social media, e-mail, and texting play a role in our temptation to react rather than respond?

With 24/7 access to social media where we can post and reply instantly to what someone has said, it can be tempting to hide behind a keyboard and react. Without hearing someone's tone in a face-to-face encounter, we can do much damage that we can't take back. Has anyone else wished there was a way to "unsend" a text?

If you are in a situation currently where you are trying to figure out the motives of another, take a moment to ask God to help you sort through your perception and reality. Reflect on any insights He gives you into determining fact and fiction in your mental gymnastics about a person or situation.

My perception of how things are in my relationship with

_____ is:

As I put myself in the other person's shoes, is there anything I might be missing because of assumptions I have made about this person?

Now ask the Lord to give you a glimpse into His greater purpose in this relationship. Is He refining you through it? Does He want to use you as His vehicle of mercy toward another? Do you need to have a good cry, like Joseph, about some painful memories or current difficulties?

Take some time to talk to God and also listen. Record below any next steps God may be calling you to make in any fragile relationships in your life:

Joseph came back after he got himself together and carried out his next steps. He had Simeon tied up to put a little fear into his brothers and motivate them to take him seriously (v. 24). Why Simeon? While we don't know for sure, we do know that Simeon was at one time a brutal man. As we learned earlier, he led the way in the murders of all the men of Shechem when his sister was raped. Perhaps it had been Simeon's cruelty that Joseph re-envisioned when he remembered being at the bottom of a pit, crying out for help. Maybe God had specifically told Joseph to pick Simeon. No matter the reason, Joseph followed through on his plans that seemed cruel at face value but, I believe, ultimately were intended to reunite his family.

I have wondered if Joseph fully processed what had happened to him and came to forgive his brothers during his prison years. If he did, why didn't he simply reveal himself and embrace his brothers at first sight? Tomorrow we will explore the concept of testing and rebuilding trust before beginning the reconciliation process. As we continue to learn from Joseph's example, may we be careful to remember his rule of response. In order to see God's bigger plan and give time for emotions to settle, we must learn to wait before taking action so that we can be responders instead of reactors.

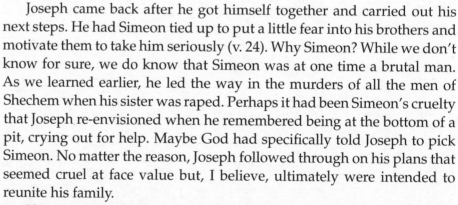

In order to see God's bigger plan and give time for emotions to settle, we must learn to wait before taking action so that we can be responders instead of reactors.

Talk with God

As we close today, consider your track record with reactions and responses. Would close friends, coworkers, or family members label you a reactor or a responder? What factors typically contribute to whether you react or respond? Write your responses in the margin.

You may find that you react to certain people and respond to others. Also, the time of day, the amount of sleep you've had, the events leading up to an encounter, and the amount of time you have spent in God's Word and prayer can influence your ability to respond. Spend some time in God's presence, asking Him to help you learn to be an even better responder. Is there a situation He is asking you to follow the rule of response by waiting twenty-four hours—or possibly even three days—before deciding what you will say or do? Lay any current situations at His feet and listen for His voice of direction or correction.

Read Through Joseph's Family Story:

Read Genesis 28–29.

Day 5: Testing before Trusting

Some people aren't "safe." In her book *Friendships of Women*, Dee Brestin compares relationships to roses and says that all roses have thorns. She writes, "After experiencing a few jabs into your soft, tender flesh, you handle roses with more respect. A dedicated rose gardener, one who believes that the glory of the rose more than compensates for the occasional wounds it inflicts, learns to bear the pain and to handle roses in such a way that she is seldom injured."[9] When we engage in deep relationships with friends, occasionally we will hit a thorn and need to reconcile. This is a normal aspect of every relationship.

Brestin also describes some women as alligators. They can inflict wounds that go beyond surface scratches, leaving scars from their bites. She explains, "Alligators demonstrate a *pattern of destruction*. Every rose has a few thorns, but an alligator is covered with them."[10] This applies to men as well. Such people are not "safe" and should be regarded with caution.

Joseph recognized his brothers in Genesis 42, but he didn't immediately reveal himself and embrace them. He needed to determine whether they would continue their alligator behavior from the past or be safe to rebuild trust after two decades of change. In our study next week, we will see him put his brothers through even more tests that almost look like games. Joseph exercised caution and tested them in order to see if it would be safe to let his guard down and reveal his true identity.

Recall some of the things Joseph's brothers did to him in the past:

Put yourself in Joseph's shoes and ask yourself these questions: What would I have done upon seeing my brothers again? Would I have ignored them and tried to forget them? Would I reveal myself to punish them? Would I test things out to ascertain the wisdom of trusting them with my new family's safety? Write your thoughts below:

Turn to Genesis 42 and fill in the blanks as we review the decisions Joseph has made so far as he has encountered his brothers:

First, he called them _____ who came only to see the weakness of the land. (v. 9)

Then he put them all in _____ for three days. (v. 17)

Next he listened to their accounts of his past and went to _____ alone. (v. 24)

Eventually, he tied up one of his brothers named _____ and let the rest return home to get their youngest brother. (v. 24)

Today we will finish reading Genesis 42 as we conclude our week of looking at dreams coming true in Joseph's life.

Read Genesis 42:25-38. In the story that the brothers tell their father in verses 30-34, do you note any details that are rearranged or left out from the account as told in verses 6-23?

The brothers claimed to be honest men, but they certainly didn't recount to their father their comments about believing these events were retribution for what they did to Joseph years earlier.

Joseph needed to determine his brothers' character. He hadn't seen them in so long, and he had changed much over the course of time while serving in Potiphar's house, enduring prison, and serving as a royal official under Pharaoh. Now he needed to see what his brothers were like. When he was seventeen, he didn't realize how unsafe they were until he was pleading with them from the bottom of a pit. He wouldn't make the same mistake again. So he set up opportunities to test them and evaluate whether he could reconcile with them and invite his wife and children into relationship with them. While he tested to see if the brothers merely had thorns or continued to be alligators, it appears that he sought God's wisdom for each step of discovery.

Throughout Joseph's story, we see his focus and faith in the God of his father, Jacob. We also get a hint in Genesis 42 of his brothers' view of this same God.

According to Genesis 42:21-22, how do the brothers seem to view God?

What question do they ask about God in verse 28?

Joseph's brothers appear to believe in a God who is punitive. They tied their past bad deeds to current misfortune. One scholar says of Joseph's brothers, "They are bound by the power of an unforgiven past, immobilized by guilt, and driven by anxiety."[11]

My friend Deanna came from a rigid religious background. When her friend Owen began sharing with her about a God of love and forgiveness, she was intrigued. She grew up thinking that God seemed like a mad father pointing His finger at her. She knew that in the past she had made choices that didn't please God, so she figured He probably was angry with her. When she understood the gospel of Christ, she embraced it and found new hope and grace in a relationship with Him. Her perception of God had been similar to the punitive God that Joseph's brothers envisioned. Though Proverbs 1:31 says that we must sometimes eat the bitter fruit of living our own way, we do not serve a punishing God. He isn't out to get us.

Have you ever thought that God was looking for opportunities to punish or point a finger at you? If so, why did you believe this?

If you no longer believe this, what has helped to reorient your view of God toward the merciful and loving God that He is?

Listening to worship music, discussing God's Word in a Bible study, listening to sermons, memorizing Scripture, and finding godly mentors with a healthy view of God are the things that continually help me refine a more biblical picture of God. He is merciful and loving. Psalm 103:8 says, "The LORD is compassionate and merciful, / slow to get angry and filled with unfailing love."

Though Joseph seems to have trusted this God of mercy in his own life, he must have thought it would be wise to test his brothers before fully trusting them. In Genesis 42:15-16, the writer twice uses the Hebrew word *bachan* (sometimes spelled *bahan*), which means "tested."[12] One source notes, "What is distinctive of *bahan* is the metallurgical connotation."[13] Fire was used in metallurgy to test metals for their quality. "So *bahan* means to test in the sense of determining or finding out the value of something. That is what Joseph is doing."[14] Just as silver was put in the fire to see if it was real, Joseph put his brothers in the fire to see if their character had changed. He wanted to see his father and his younger brother Benjamin, but he also wanted to determine if his brothers are safe. Can they establish a relationship of some sort? To what extent can they reconcile? He is testing the possibilities.

Sometimes we can be too quick to reconnect after experiencing pain in a relationship. If we reestablish trust without testing for safety first, we can end up losing a relationship for lack of proper boundaries. We must be careful not to excuse as thorns the blows of alligators. Through listening to many stories of forgiveness, I have found that some people can be unsafe for us, depending on our interactions and histories, yet still be flowers in someone else's garden.

Consider Mary's story of relationship testing and ultimately finding the need for stronger boundaries in order to prioritize her marriage:

> My husband and I attended the same church for over thirty years. It's where we met, married, and raised all three of our children. I love these people as if they are my own family. My husband and I served the church in many capacities over the years, including my husband using his maintenance skills as a love gift. Three years ago he was deeply hurt as his motives for serving were called into question. He resigned from his official responsibilities and basically stopped attending.
>
> I continued in my role as a ministry team leader and pushed back the feelings of hurt. I was encouraged by my children and a dear friend who is a psychologist to confront the leaders, but I was afraid that I wouldn't get the response I needed and would have to leave the church. And I just couldn't do that. It would be too much of a loss.

So for three years I pressed on in ministry and watched my husband become more and more bitter. Finally, the Holy Spirit started pulling on my heart. When I couldn't resist any longer, I set up a meeting with the leaders and shared my heart about how my husband was treated. Basically I was told that it was all him and that they had done nothing wrong. There was no compassion, no stepping back to evaluate their own actions.

It was clear to me that I had to leave my church family. I told my husband about my decision, and we decided to go to a new church. I can't put into words what it has been like to see the positive changes and spiritual growth in my husband. We've committed to wait a year before getting involved in serving again, but we can't wait to do so.

Mary's story includes a painful journey of waiting, seeking counsel, and testing waters. It reminds us that every story has two sides, and we must wrestle to reconcile our perspectives with those of the others involved. It also shows that although we can always forgive, we can't always reconcile. Reconciliation takes two willing, humble parties.

Describe a time when you have tested to evaluate whether a particular relationship fell into the *rose with thorns* or *alligator* category.

How did the time of testing reveal the character of the individual?

Joseph had been tested through the fire of adversity to reveal the quality of his character. He needed to do the same with his brothers to see how they would handle injustice and to ascertain if they would display integrity and loyalty toward Benjamin. This would be key information in knowing whether he could trust them with his true identity.

Under pressure, our true natures are exposed. When conflict or difficulty puts our relationships to the test, we must seek God's help to determine whether our pain is simply a surface scratch or an alligator bite so that we can know what next steps to take. Next week we will explore this topic further as Joseph begins the roller coaster ride of reconciliation.

Read Through Joseph's Family Story:

Read Genesis 30.

Talk with God

As we close this week, consider what God might be saying to you through our week of study in Genesis 41–42. If your time is limited, ask God the following questions without going back to the text. If you have a few extra minutes, read back through Genesis 41–42 as you ask God these questions:

- God, what are you trying to teach me about Your character?
- What insights can You give me about the nature of people?
- Is there anything You are trying to teach me in my current relationships/ circumstances?

End with a prayer, thanking God that sometimes dreams do come true. Thank God for any dreams that have come to pass in your life and for what He has been teaching you this week through the Joseph narrative.

Digging Deeper

God gave Pharaoh two dreams to confirm his message. What is the significance of the doubles we see consistently throughout Joseph's story? . Check out the Digging Deeper article for Week 3, "The Power of Two," for some insight into these pairings and the significance they have for us (see AbingdonPress.com/Joseph).

Dreams Coming True

God can use the pain in our lives to build _____ _____.

Staying _____ and _____ will help us pass the test of power.

_____ *goes before destruction,*

    and haughtiness before a fall. (Proverbs 16:18)

When Joseph came face-to-face with his offenders, he exercised

_____.

R _____.

A _____.

P _____.

Week 4

THE ROLLER COASTER RIDE

Genesis 43–44

Memory Verse

"And now, dear brothers and sisters, one final thing. Fix your thoughts on what is true, and honorable, and right, and pure, and lovely, and admirable. Think about things that are excellent and worthy of praise."

(Philippians 4:8)

Day 1: Withholding in a Famine

When we sat outside on a beautiful morning with cups of tea, I listened intently as Marilyn talked about her journey to forgiveness and reconciliation. She used the illustration of a roller coaster ride—with ups and downs, highs and lows—to describe how she felt throughout the journey. Marilyn's story began with her father, a first-generation Christian who escaped a childhood of abuse when he embraced the gospel of Christ. He went into full-time ministry on a Navajo reservation. Marilyn looked up to her father as the man who taught her about the Lord and gained the trust of the Navaho people through many years of faithful service.

Marilyn later married a pastor, and they raised their own children to know and love God. Imagine her shock when, after her parents retired, lawsuits for inappropriate contact with a child were brought against her father in two states. She didn't know what to believe. When her father admitted to the truth of some of the allegations, she felt angry, hurt, and deceived. Her father's sin left so many repercussions in its wake. She now faced many decisions about what she would say, do, and think in the months and years of heartache ahead. A situation she had no control over now would test her character and rock her family relationships.

As I drove away in my car, I knew I had been in the presence of one of God's unsung heroes. Marilyn's story of the ups and downs of forgiveness and of reestablishing trust is so powerful that we will explore a part of it each day this week as a modern, feminine counterpart alongside Joseph's similar roller coaster ride of reconciliation.

This week we will see Joseph as an active participant in both the forgiveness and reconciliation process with his brothers. It is important to note that forgiveness is not the same thing as reconciliation.

We are always called to forgive others through the power of God working in our lives. To forgive, we acknowledge the hurt and strong emotions that accompany the pain and then ask God to help us freely let go of the offense. The Hebrew word for forgive is *nasa*, which means "to lift up."[1] When we forgive, we lift up the pain to God and require no penance or payment from our offender. Forgiveness takes only one person and happens on the inside of a person.

Fun Fact:

Scholars estimate that two years passed between the first return of Joseph's brothers from Egypt, when they had the grain and money in their sacks, and their departure back to Egypt to face Joseph.

Reconciliation, on the other hand, takes two people. Only after both parties have repented of any wrongdoing toward the other can they come close again in relationship. After reconciliation, the relationship may be even better than before the offense or may require new boundaries, depending on how both parties behave after they have reunited.

The process to both forgiveness and reconciliation is not clear-cut and differs from person to person. In other words, there is not one right way. Sometimes we forgive quickly and then spend a long time reconciling. Other times we struggle with forgiveness forever and then quickly reconcile. And sometimes we make it to forgiveness but not to reconciliation. There are as many different scenarios as there are roller coaster rides.

As we pick up Joseph's story this week, we find the harsh famine years greatly impacting his father and brothers' families in Canaan. Just as Marilyn had no control over what came to light about her father, these families are at the mercy of a widespread famine. The rain isn't falling, whether they like it or not.

Are you facing a situation that you have no control over right now? What famine in your life is causing you to feel dry and limited?

The famine has become a life-and-death predicament that this family cannot ignore as the food supply they brought from Egypt continues to diminish.

Turn to Genesis 43 and read verses 1-14. Who are the two men dialoguing in this passage?

Joseph's father, Jacob, is now a shell of the man who had tricked his twin brother out of the birthright and blessing, deeply loved Rachel while ending up with Leah in the morning, and wrestled with God. He had succeeded and failed in trusting the God of his father Isaac and grandfather Abraham. Let's dig a little deeper to see what we can learn and apply from his attitude and actions in these verses.

Turn back to Genesis 42:36-38, and check any of the following statements that Jacob made after his sons informed him about their encounter in Egypt and the need to return there:

__ I would die if anything happens to Benjamin.
__ Everything is going against me.
__ Go back and get Simeon and more food, and we will trust God to protect Benjamin.

Here we find Jacob withholding out of fear. He won't give up his favorite son, Benjamin.

We see throughout Scripture that God is as concerned with our inaction as He is with our action. When biblical men and women failed to discipline their children, get rid of idols, or leave their comfort zones in order to obey God, consequences ensued that echoed for generations.

Silence can speak louder than any words spoken. It can communicate neglect and a lack of care, doing great harm to people we love. When I hear people tell about their childhood hurts, they often refer to what wasn't done. They weren't told they were loved, parents didn't come to their school events, or some other important thing they needed wasn't given. Withholding can cause deep pain.

Can you think of a situation, person, or thing that you are fearfully holding on to when God is asking you to release it to Him? (Think of people, finances, feelings, or positions—especially if you are in a season of famine.)

Jacob holds out as long as he can. He is focused only on what he might lose rather than on all he has to gain.

What does Jacob stand to lose by sending his sons back to Egypt?

What does he stand to gain?

Even with the possibility of obtaining food, Simeon's freedom, and more blessings than he could ever imagine, Jacob doesn't want to take a risk. He can't see past the possibility of loss. I can identify with Jacob when I'm holding on in fear instead of moving ahead in faith. How about you? Perhaps seeing how withholding worked out for Jacob will inspire us to make a move toward obedience.

1. Jacob holds on to unrealistic expectations.

Jacob's reluctance to let go leads to unrealistic expectations. One commentator writes, "Jacob casually requests his sons to return to Egypt to get *a little more corn* as if Egypt is a tad down the road, a place where one can make a quick trip to purchase odds and ends."[2] Perhaps Jacob has convinced himself that he can send his other sons but withhold Benjamin, concocting a dream world in which he can have the benefits of obedience without the sacrifice. When we withhold, we tend to minimize.

Jacob knows good and well that they can't go without Benjamin, but it's too painful to consider. Even when Judah offers his life to protect Benjamin, Jacob doesn't want to accept the offer.

When I'm feeling stuck like Jacob, I often will shoot down every possibility someone suggests. I would rather cling to unrealistic expectations.

Recall the situation, person, or thing you identified that you are holding on to in fear instead of releasing to God in faith. Can you think of any unrealistic expectations you might have related to this situation, person, or thing? List any that come to mind:

Ask God if He might want you to have a conversation with coworkers, friends, or family about any unrealistic expectations you might have of them. This is a big step in moving beyond our fear.

Judah confronted Jacob about his unrealistic expectations. This led Jacob to another pitfall of walking by fear instead of faith.

2. Jacob blames others.

When Judah exposes Jacob's unrealistic expectations by reminding him of the very specific and strict condition that the Egyptian ruler had given them, Jacob responds with a verbal attack.

Notice what Jacob says in 43:6. Write his question here:

When the famine and personal circumstances in his life become overwhelming, Jacob blames others. He has the choice to obey and release Benjamin or to maintain his inaction. Both have consequences.

Who or what becomes a target for you when you feel overwhelmed?

You are not alone. We all have this tendency, but let's not allow ourselves to stay in blaming mode. Next time we hear whispers of blame in our thoughts and words, let's recognize it and choose a different response. Famines come into our lives and can tempt us to point our finger at others. However, we can overcome our tendency to blame by shifting our focus away from self and fix our gaze on God. Only then can we begin taking personal responsibility and trusting God instead.

Jacob demonstrates one more characteristic of withholding and living in fear that we need to be careful to avoid.

3. Jacob is paralyzed by grief.

Sometimes life's great famines can be paralyzing. I can't imagine how Marilyn must have felt when she put the phone down after hearing the allegations against her father. We can get weak in the knees when relational tension threatens to tear our family apart. Jacob certainly did.

Loss has left Jacob afraid and stuck. The lack in his life is blinding him momentarily from trusting in God. One scholar suggests that "his feelings of grief and despair had almost extinguished his faith."[3] The struggle for survival often brings to the surface a deep wrestling with faith. As we study the roller coaster ride of reconciliation, we find Jacob unwilling to get on the ride. In his old age, he knows the highs and lows and risks involved. It's scary. He doesn't want any thrills—just safety.

As I get older, I find safety climbing higher on my priority list. I tend to want the path of least relational strife. This is why I love the picture God gives us of Jacob. He actually doesn't come to trust God until he has to. It makes me think of a verse in Psalm 40: "Now that you have *made* me listen, I finally understand" (v. 6, emphasis added).

Sometimes God puts up with our withholding only for a season, and then He places us in a situation where we have to move. Our human emotions mix with faith that God will take care of us. Fear and faith collide until one wins out.

The need for bread and the fear of what could happen to his sons and grandchildren finally lead Jacob to faith—perhaps mixed with resignation. I like what one commentator says about him in this passage: "It is difficult to know where faith leaves off and cynical resignation sets in."[4]

Can you relate to cynical resignation? I can. Jacob can let everyone starve in his state of stuck-ness, or he can choose to trust God. He has only those two options. Ultimately, he chooses to believe despite his fear. Likewise, we often must act despite our fear.

Look again at Genesis 43:14. What name does Jacob use for God in this verse?

The name translated "God Almighty" is *El Shaddai* in Hebrew. It means "the All-Sufficient One."[5] This is the name God had revealed to Jacob earlier in his life after changing his name to Israel: "Then God said, "I am El-Shaddai—'God Almighty.' Be fruitful and multiply. You will become a great nation, even many nations. Kings will be among your descendants!" (Genesis 35:11). In Jacob's grief, he had lost sight of God's promise. Now he finally lays aside his unrealistic expectations, blame, and paralyzing grief and embraces the All-Sufficient One.

It's interesting to note that in 43:11 when he concedes to release Benjamin, he is referred to as *Israel* rather than *Jacob*. One source explains, "'Jacob' represents the suffering, human, feeling side of the patriarch, while 'Israel' is used to underscore the office and the dignity of the patriarch."[6] It is Israel who finally assumes his mantle of leadership and issues seven imperatives, instructing his sons in what to take on their journey.

Like Jacob, we too can easily forget God's great promises to be all that we need. Essentially we have the same options. We can choose bitterness, or we can grow through grief and prepare to follow God. And here's the good news: we can choose to follow God even if…

- we trust Him only after exhausting every other option we have.
- we are still scared to release something or someone.
- our faith resembles cynical resignation.

Write your own "even if" statement below:

I can choose to trust God even if _____.

> *Such love has no fear, because perfect love expels all fear. If we are afraid, it is for fear of punishment, and this shows that we have not fully experienced his perfect love.*
>
> *(1 John 4:18)*

We can put our trust in the All-Sufficient One "even if" we still have some humanness to work through. We are going to see that even in Jacob's brokenness and loss and struggle, God shows up in a big way.

Read 1 John 4:18 in the margin, and write below what God says will expel fear.

This perfect love comes from our All-Sufficient One, who longs to bless us. Despite Jacob's fear, God has plans to bless him. One commentator writes, "God, through the famine initiates the saving process by forcing the family to confront their past and each other."[7] God uses the very thing that seems to be the source of the problem—the famine—as the path to reconciliation.

Today God is calling you to release your tight fist and trust His perfect love. Take a moment to think about what you are withholding. Forgiveness? A move? A job change? An apology? Understanding? A person? Whatever "it" is—hold out your palm right now and picture it there. Close your fist tight over it and admit to God that it's hard to let it go. Speak honestly with Him. Tell Him all about your pain.

Now, open your fist and lift your hand up to God. Choose today to give it to Him. Remember that this process is like a roller coaster ride with ups and downs, so you might need to do it again in an hour, and tomorrow, and the next day. But every time it comes to your mind, close your fist, open your palm, and lift it up. Let this be a symbolic act between you and God that helps you remember He is the All-Sufficient One who longs to bless you—even during times of famine.

I'm so excited to be on this journey to forgiveness with you. Joseph's story is only going to grow more intense throughout the week, so we will need to fasten our seatbelts. This roller coaster ride of reconciliation is going to have some pretty significant highs and lows as we leave Jacob behind in Canaan and watch Joseph put his brothers through multiple "inversions" to see if they can be trusted.

God wants to draw near to you through all the ups and downs in your own journey with forgiveness and reconciliation. We serve a God who is an expert at forgiveness and longs to help through every twist and turn.

Talk with God

Complete the prayer to God below, and then spend some time listening for what He has to say to you. Write anything you hear in the space provided.

God, You are the All-Sufficient One. Your love is perfect. My famine right now looks like this: _____.

Please help me to overcome the human defaults of unrealistic expectations, blaming, and paralyzing grief. I especially need your help with _____.

Show me how to trust You by faith and let go of what I've been withholding from You and others.

Speak Your truth over me right now. I'm listening. Amen.

Day 2: Buckle Up

Yesterday we met Marilyn and heard how her roller coaster ride began when her father received legal accusations of inappropriate contact with

children in two states. As the official proceedings started, she and her siblings rallied together with their mother to plan a family meeting where the intent of forgiveness was verbalized to her repentant father. Marilyn admitted that she really struggled in her prayer and thought life during this time. She would fly from the Midwest, leaving her husband and children, to represent their family at court hearings in the West. One minute she would want harsh punishment for her dad when she thought about the victims and the pain he had caused. Other times she would ask God for mercy and gentleness toward him as he repented and wept.

Her traveling and anguish also put a financial and emotional strain on her husband and children. At times she would be resentful about the consequences her father's sin had brought in her own life. She had to discipline herself to look for the good in the midst of all the bad, such as a person who anonymously left money on her doorstep. Over time she realized God was showing her that although she hadn't committed the crimes her father had, she also was a sinner. She had lied; she had broken God's law; she had made mistakes too. Yet God had fully and freely forgiven her. She grew deeper with God through all her questions and grief.

This is our theme for today's lesson as we finish Chapter 43 of Genesis: God gives us treasure even in the midst of struggles in our relationships.

Read Genesis 43:15-34. Then, starting with the lowest blank and working up, write every good thing that happens to the brothers in the verses indicated. Two have been done for you.

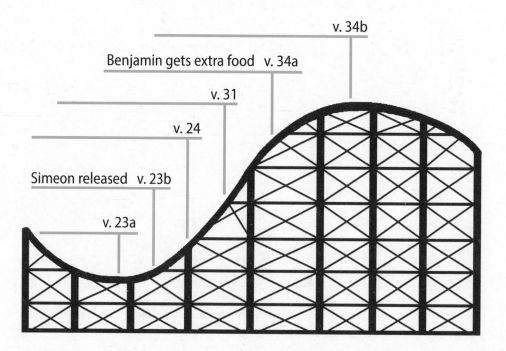

v. 34b

Benjamin gets extra food   v. 34a

v. 31

v. 24

Simeon released   v. 23b

v. 23a

We see that as the brothers arrive in town and find out they are invited to Joseph's house, they are terrified. Just as their father feared losing Benjamin, they are fearful that the money they found in their sacks after their previous trip has now brought them big trouble. I imagine them rehearsing an explanation about why they didn't come back right away once they discovered the money. I would think that Joseph watched for his brothers almost daily once sufficient time for them to return home and come back had elapsed. Once again he had to trust in God's sovereign timing.

The brothers might have thought they had missed the window to get Simeon out of prison and buy more food from this ruler in Egypt. Can't you imagine their fear escalating as they wait for him in his home? Perhaps they thought, *What if he won't give us food? What if he kills us all?* After all, this ruler had been harsh to them last time, even accusing them as spies. No wonder they were reluctant to return.

I can relate. There have been times when I have been tempted to think I have reached the point of no return in relationships, believing that too much time has passed to reconnect or reconcile.

Have you ever thought that it was too late to reconcile a relationship? If so, describe the situation below.

There is no statute of limitations on reconciliation. Reconciliation itself takes time, and it is never too late to make it right.

What does Matthew 19:26 (in the margin) assure us?

> *Jesus looked at them intently and said, "Humanly speaking, it is impossible. But with God everything is possible."*
>
> *(Matthew 19:26)*

Joseph is now more than thirty-seven years old, so at least twenty years have passed since his brothers sold him into slavery. Yet as we see, it's never too late or too hard for God.

Whether the brothers feel guilty about the lapse of time since discovering the money in their sacks or have been taught that it's better to fess up than to be found out, they go to the steward with the truth. In the steward's response we again see a reminder of God's hand in the timing and details of a family saga that seems nonsensical to those living it out. One commentator writes, "Unwittingly the steward expresses one of the central themes of the book: 'the God of your father has given you treasure' (v. 23)."[9] The Hebrew word used here is *matmon* (treasure), not *kesep* (money). The writer uses a word that is more dramatic—one that "refers specifically to buried treasure."[10]

Can you identify some of the good things God is doing in the midst of your current struggles? If so, name them below.

Has some of this "treasure" been buried? In what ways have you had to "dig deep" to see God's treasure in the midst of your own personal times of famine?

The incident with the money is part of the testing Joseph is putting his brothers through before trusting them again. What will they do about the money in their sacks? Will they lead with honesty? Will they make excuses? Will they avoid the subject or deny it? In this case, the brothers show integrity. I like to think that Joseph is cheering inside, thinking that perhaps he will be able to reveal himself and reunite with his brothers after all. However, he wisely waits for the right time. For now, the charade continues.

Though good things are happening circumstantially for the brothers, there is still a missing piece—authenticity. While they eat and celebrate together, there is a big elephant in the room that hasn't been addressed. Not only is Joseph's identity still hidden, but also the brothers have not repented. Repentance must precede reconciliation. We will talk more about that issue in tomorrow's lesson. For now, let's consider two important cautions we learn from this scene.

First, we must be careful not to measure success in relationships by a lack of conflict or difficulty. And second, we must not confuse counterfeit happiness with the lasting joy of reconciliation. Once we move beyond our paralyzing grief and board the ride toward reconciliation, we find ourselves enjoying the climb. One thing after another seems to be falling into place. This is where Joseph's brothers find themselves. They had been used to rationing food, but now they find themselves feasting at a royal table. The man who spoke harshly to them before seems to be providing for their every need. They have Simeon back and can buy more grain to take home to their families.

This is only a step in the process, however, not the end of the ride. Warren Wiersbe writes, "This was a false and transient joy, because the brothers had not yet dealt with their sins. It's one thing to be relieved and quite something else to be forgiven and reconciled.... To experience false joy and peace is a perilous thing, and to think that we're right with God because life is easier and problems less threatening is to court disaster."[11]

Look up these two passages and summarize each one briefly:

Proverbs 14:12

Deuteronomy 30:19

One of the prevalent themes in Genesis 43 and 44, our chapters this week, is the contrast between life and death. When it comes to relationships, we need to be sure we are making choices that will lead to life. I once heard a preacher say that often what we feel like doing in a relationship is the opposite of what we actually should do.

I think that when Joseph saw Benjamin, he must have wanted to hug him tight and say, "I'm not dead; let's lose these other guys and celebrate." It must have taken restraint not to do that, knowing he needed to finish testing the waters before he could trust. Instead, Joseph ran out of the room, let his emotions run their course, and then pulled himself together. He must have been looking at the bigger picture of long-term trust rather than short-term gratification. In a sense, he was faced with a choice that could lead to life or death in his relationship with his brothers, and he chose life.

We experience life or death choices in relationships every day, and how we want to respond in our flesh does not lead to life and vitality. Often it leads to death—of trust, intimacy, or even any contact at all. But just as there is a path that leads to death, so there is a path that leads to life. If we feel like getting even, then we can show love. If we feel like withholding affection, then we can write an encouraging note. If we feel like saying a harsh word, then we can give a gentle answer or take a time out.

Make a couple of if/then statements that are relevant to your life and relationships right now:

If I feel like _____,

then I can _____.

If I feel like _____,

then I can _____.

Is there a specific word, action, or attitude you need to change in order to promote life instead of death in one of your relationships?

In every relationship, we are either moving toward or away from closeness. There are highs and there are lows. Every marriage, sibling relationship, and deep friendship has times of climbing and seeing the heights—meals shared, times of celebration, abundance—but these highs are not the measure of intimacy and reconciliation. This counterfeit happiness will not compare with the joy of reconciliation yet to come.

Even so, the high moments are to be appreciated. For Joseph and his brothers, this high moment they share is a gift.

Reread Genesis 43:26. What happens in this verse?

Here we see the fulfillment of Joseph's dream. All eleven brothers bow down to him. Then God gives Joseph the opportunity to observe and serve his brothers, and they enjoy a time of feasting together. One source notes that the Hebrew literally reads, "They drank and got drunk with him."[12]

We've seen Joseph move toward closeness by blessing his brothers and setting their minds at ease. Tomorrow comes the real test when the coaster begins its descent at rapid speeds. Sometimes things get worse before they can get better on the road to reconciliation. In those times, God calls us to dig for the buried treasure of His grace, which is always within reach.

Talk with God

Let's end today by thanking God for giving us some climbs to high points along the way to encourage us. Even if they are temporary and superficial at times, they give us a break from what can feel like one hard thing after another. In the margin, write as many small joys in your current relationships as you can think of today.

Thank God that He is working in your life and that He has treasure for you even in the midst of struggles. Sometimes it's buried under layers of heartache, but if you will stay the course, follow His lead, and keep your eyes focused on Him, you will see your God-sized dreams come true just as Joseph did.

Day 3: Whiplash from the Ups and Downs

Marilyn encountered a test on her roller coaster of forgiveness when she was asked to speak in court on her father's behalf. She could talk a good forgiveness game, but could she get on a plane and put feet to forgiveness, speaking well of her dad publicly? Never before in her life had she faced such an agonizing decision. She cried the entire plane ride as she wrestled with her own humanness and God's supernatural commands.

Talking about forgiveness is much easier than actually living it out. Yet when she walked off the plane, she felt complete peace. In the end, it wasn't necessary for her to share her statement. However, the lawyer read it to her father privately. Later that day her father leaned over to her and asked, "Why are you doing this for me?" She was able to share with him that she had learned forgiveness from him. He had taught her about Christ—the greatest forgiver of all time, the author of the gospel of grace. In his book *What's So Amazing About Grace?* Philip Yancey writes, "The gospel of grace begins and ends with forgiveness. And people write songs with titles like 'Amazing Grace' for one reason: grace is the only force in the universe powerful enough to break the chains that enslave generations. Grace alone melts ungrace."[13]

Today we find the brothers leaving Egypt for home with a sigh of relief only to find themselves in deep trouble again. Joseph puts them through a puzzling scenario.

Read Genesis 44:1-17 and then label the descent of the roller coaster, summing up each bad thing that happened to the brothers as they were aware of it. I've done the first one for you—because for me the first bad thing would have been waking up at dawn!

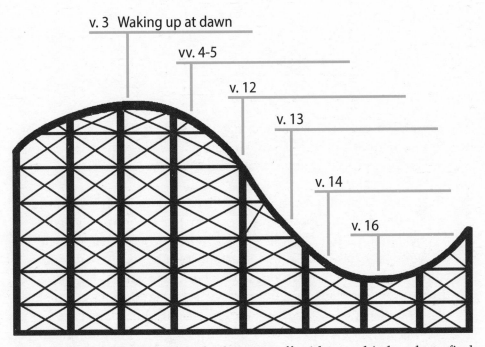

v. 3 Waking up at dawn

vv. 4-5

v. 12

v. 13

v. 14

v. 16

The brothers thought they had gotten off without a hitch only to find their worst fears realized.

Fun Fact:

The form of divination referred to in Genesis 44 is either oleomancy (oil poured into water) or hydromancy (water poured into oil). Diviners would look for configurations in the mixture of oil and water and make interpretations based on what they observed.[14]

Can you think of a time when a relationship was starting to mend and then things got really complicated again? What happened in your circumstance?

While we can make charts and organize facts on paper, the messy tangle of emotions, comments, and past memories all contribute to the ups and downs in the process of true reconciliation. Forgiveness takes only one person, but reconciliation takes at least two. Tomorrow we will consider how Joseph is testing his brothers. Today our focus is on Joseph's personal struggle with extending grace.

Take another look at verses 1-17. Are there elements of the story that are puzzling for you?

For me, I'm confused by Joseph employing the pagan practice of using a diviner's cup in his methods. I also wonder why Joseph sets up this scenario rather than directly addressing his brothers. What is Joseph's intent?

Imagine for a moment that you are Joseph—with all the power of Egypt behind you. What might you have had in mind with this charade of hiding the silver cup?

Though we can only surmise what Joseph is thinking and feeling, I believe it's possible that his shenanigans are part of his own inner grappling with grace. No one says it better than Philip Yancey:

When I was a child listening to the story in Sunday school, I could not understand the loops and twists in the account of Joseph's reconciliation with his brothers. One moment Joseph acted harshly, throwing his brothers in jail; the next moment he seemed overcome with sorrow, leaving the room to blubber like a drunk. He played tricks on his brothers, hiding money in their grain sacks, seizing one as a hostage, accusing another of stealing his silver cup. For months, maybe years, these intrigues dragged on until finally Joseph could restrain himself no longer. He summoned his brothers and dramatically forgave them.

I now see that story as a realistic depiction of the unnatural act of forgiveness. The brothers Joseph struggled to forgive were the very ones who had bullied him, had cooked up schemes to murder him, and sold him into slavery. Because of them he had spent the best years of his youth moldering in an Egyptian dungeon. Though he went on to triumph over adversity and though with all his heart he now wanted to forgive these brothers, he could not bring himself to that point, not yet. The wound still hurt too much.[15]

The concepts of grace and forgiveness are unnatural to live out. We can easily talk about them and agree they are God's way, but when it comes to actually looking at our betrayer with love, it's no easy ride. I have wished my mind could be free of negative thoughts that continue to recur about individuals who have caused me pain. When we don't care about people, it doesn't hurt so much. In contrast, when we have trusted others with our hearts, secrets, and love, the pain of rejection and betrayal isn't easily wished away.

I asked a question on social media about who is hardest to forgive:

A) The martyr who always sees herself as the victim
B) The judger who acts like she is never wrong
C) The excuser who always has a reason for why she hurt others

I got more responses to this question than anything I had posted that week. So many of us are riding the roller coaster of pain.

How would you answer? Circle one of the choices above.

I ask this question because I believe understanding where we lack grace can help us be more intentional in offering it. We may not even realize we easily forgive the excuser but have no grace for the martyr. When we know where we struggle, we can ask Jesus to help us give His grace freely to *all*, not just to the easy ones. Joseph's brothers included jealous rivals, kidnappers, liars, and even murderers. (The martyr, judger, and excuser aren't looking so bad anymore, are they?)

Forgiveness isn't easy, especially with those who aren't saying they are sorry. One person responded to my question with this comment: "None of the above—the one who betrayed me, because I trusted him/her. All of Joseph's brothers betrayed him. Ask anyone who has felt that pain. It cuts deep." Joseph's pain certainly wasn't a surface wound. He was even thinking of his brothers' betrayal when he named his children. His journey toward forgiveness and reconciliation was a roller coaster of ups and downs.

Let's look at some of Joseph's antics and their connections to what his brothers did to him back in the day.

Read the Scriptures indicated to fill out this chart. State what Joseph's brothers did to him in the left column. Then write a similar action that he did to them in the right column. I have done the first one for you because there what happened to Joseph is an assumed probability, not a fact stated in the text.

What happened to Joseph?	What happened to Joseph's brothers?
Genesis 37:2 Accused of being a spy	Genesis 42:9 Accused of being spies
Genesis 37:4	Genesis 42:30
Genesis 39:13-15	Genesis 44:4-5
Genesis 39:20	Genesis 42:17

Do you think that Joseph consciously put his brothers through struggles similar to those that he had experienced? If so, why do you think he did this?

Now think about your own journey to forgiveness, and describe a time when you wished your pain on the person who had caused it in your life (whether you acted on it or not).

Forgiveness is a journey where we wrestle against our human tendencies toward retribution, unforgiveness, and bitterness. Philip Yancey writes, "Behind every act of forgiveness lies a wound of betrayal and the pain of being betrayed does not easily fade away."[16] Lewis Smedes described the pain as a nettle in our minds, saying that "the only way to remove the nettle is with a surgical procedure called forgiveness."[17] Joseph struggled with forgiveness just as we do, yet we will find him coming to the point of grace. We, too, can get there, but not without a roller coaster ride. It may be a small one like the Seven Dwarfs Mine Train at Disney World, or it may be a large one that is dark and scary at times like Space Mountain. The ultimate goal is to work through the pain and follow Jesus to the freedom of forgiveness—and when possible, to reconciliation. Forgiveness is the only remedy to the pain.

Marilyn spoke about how one moment she wanted mercy for her dad and other days she thought only of justice and consequences. Can you relate to similar ups and downs in your thoughts when struggling to forgive?

Think of a past or present struggle with forgiveness, and label the roller coaster below with two positive and two negative thoughts, words, or actions that have been part of the ride. You won't be asked to share the negatives, so be totally honest. The positives can be thoughts you dwell on, songs you listen to, positive people you call, or specific actions you take to help you move toward forgiveness.

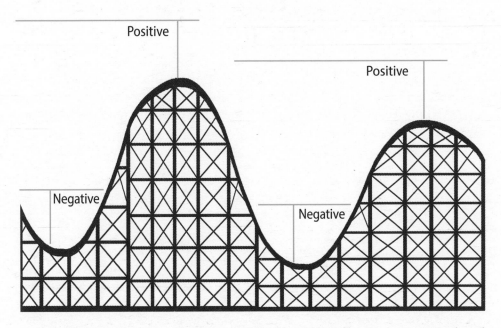

My negatives often revolve around rehearsing offenses in my mind and justifying myself, which sometimes lead me to review things the person has said or done in the past with a new judgmental bent. Some positive things for me include focusing on God's grace toward me, praying for those who have hurt or offended me, and memorizing Scripture. Marilyn mentioned that one of the most helpful things for her was setting her mind on truth.

Read Through Joseph's Family Story:

Read Genesis 34.

> *And now, dear brothers and sisters, one final thing. Fix your thoughts on what is true, and honorable, and right, and pure, and lovely, and admirable. Think about things that are excellent and worthy of praise.*
>
> *(Philippians 4:8)*

Read Philippians 4:8 in the margin and list the things God says we are to fix our minds on:

Marilyn's family certainly understood the downside of the roller coaster. She laughed as she said that at times it was almost comical; with almost everything they prayed for, the opposite seemed to happen. However, in the midst of it, they saw God give her dad a ministry to others in the prison where they had asked God not to send him. It was there that he read Scripture with his younger roommate morning and night. Her dad died in this prison after suffering some significant health challenges, leaving behind a new disciple of Christ.

How amazing God's grace is that He uses us in spite of our sin. When we repent and turn to Him, we receive grace that is truly greater than all our shortcomings. There was grace for Marilyn's dad, and there is grace for us, too—no matter what we have done.

Talk with God

The gospel truths of God's grace are a perfect place to set our minds when we are struggling with the roller coaster of thoughts and emotions related to those who have hurt us. As you prepare to talk with God, look at three amazing passages that reveal Him as the ultimate Forgiver.

Read each Scripture and write a one-sentence prayer of thanks to God beside each passage:

Psalm 103:12

Romans 5:8

1 John 1:9

Now choose one of these verses that especially encourages you and write it somewhere you can see it daily. Write it on a mirror with a dry erase marker, on an index or note card and carry it with you, or in the notes section of your phone so that you can look at it often. The next time your thoughts try to take you on the roller coaster ride of blaming, shaming, or wishing the worst on your offender, fix your mind on the gospel truths of God's great love for you and your offender.

Day 4: Making an Appeal

Fun Fact:
Judah's speech in Genesis 44 is the longest speech by a human found in the Book of Genesis.[18]

Marilyn's journey with forgiveness didn't end with her father. At the same time that she was working through those family issues, things were getting sticky with her husband's job in the church. After much prayer and reflection, her husband took an issue to the church leaders and found his to be a lone view. Marilyn and her husband loved this church body in which they and their children felt very connected to their friends and support system. Yet at the end of the day, her husband needed to resign for the sake of church unity and his own integrity.

Marilyn would say that ultimately these church forgiveness issues took her even deeper into the depths of God's grace as she struggled to process all the hurt from this least expected source. Again it was a daily battle to work through the pain and stand on the solid rock of Christ as her foundation. She found that God revealed to her what she needed to know for the moment and then said, "Trust Me for the rest." Marilyn discovered that the journey to forgiveness involves grappling with the tension between our human emotions and God's grace.

As we see the brothers being stopped outside the city, accused of stealing, and taken back to face Joseph, we realize that Joseph likewise has been struggling through his human emotions on the road to grace and forgiveness. While this test with the silver cup as well as the earlier trick with money in the brothers' sacks very much could have resulted from Joseph's struggle to show grace, they also show an element of wisdom related to testing. One source suggests, "While it had looked like he was working a slow revenge upon his brothers, we can now see that his purpose was not revenge but repentance."[19] I tend to agree that Joseph's end game was his brothers' repentance and their reconciliation as a family, yet here we see the wisdom of testing before trusting.

Discretion is something God is teaching me through Joseph's life. I often am too quick to share intimate details and not careful enough to build trust before revealing myself fully. The flip side of this is that there are times when, after being hurt, I wear a mask and don't let people see the real me.

Draw a star on the line below to indicate where you see your relationships in general (with your closest friends and family members):

Wearing a mask; hiding true feelings   Telling everything; having no filter

Let's gain some clarity about what Joseph is looking for from this time of testing.

Reread Genesis 44:14-17. What excuses did Judah offer to Joseph?

None is correct! He doesn't use any of the tactics we mentioned yesterday, complaining of unfair treatment like a martyr. He doesn't accuse Joseph or demand justice even though he isn't guilty. We also don't see the brothers shifting blame on one another or any of the royal servants.

Instead, how does Judah reply in verse 16?

He basically says, "We have nothing to say. We are sinners." How many times would our conflicts be resolved earlier and reconciliation happen sooner if we could admit that we have no explanation other than we are sinners and we are sorry? How often we overcomplicate the matter. I often do this in my marriage. I justify, argue, and want my husband to understand why I was thoughtless, rude, or inconsiderate. After almost twenty years of marriage, I'm learning to listen when I've hurt him, try to understand where he is coming from, and apologize rather than justify.

Even though Joseph has manufactured a situation with a false accusation, it's a very big step for his brothers to come to a point where they can say, "What can we say?" The brothers who schemed and manipulated in the beginning of the story are finally learning to speak simple truth.

Now we will finish Genesis 44 by reading the longest human speech given in the Book of Genesis.

Read Genesis 44:18-34. Every time Judah says either of the phrases below, make a tick mark next to the corresponding phrase:

my lord

your servant(s)

What do you notice about the tone of Judah's speech?

Judah's discourse offers us a lesson in making an appeal. And whether we realize it or not, we all make appeals in our relationships, especially with those who are closest to us.

My husband and I have tried to teach our children to respect our authority when we make a decision, but we also have left the door open for them to have a voice. From the time they were very small, we've taught them that if they feel we did not have all the information when making a decision, they can ask the question, "Can I make an appeal?" Sometimes we have amended our decision based on a new perspective, but most times we have stayed the course on our original choice. (They quickly found that when they made an appeal with no new information or logic, they only frustrated us; so they began to use appeals more sparingly.) Learning how to appeal is something we all need guidance and help with, especially when we are rebuilding a broken relationship. Consider these four principles of an appeal we learn from Judah's speech:

1. **Choose the right posture.** Judah speaks respectfully. He uses a tone and language that convey humility.
2. **Give the history and background information.** Before he makes his request, Judah spends the majority of his words (verses 18-32) helping the other party fully understand the complexity of the situation. A clear recounting of the events leading up to the present plays a great role in mutual understanding. Judah focuses more time on background before addressing the current situation. Not until verses 33-34 does he actually discuss the present circumstances.
3. **Be solution oriented.** Judah proposes a sacrificial possibility to address the issue: he offers himself in Benjamin's place, playing the role of redeemer. It's easy to point out a problem, but finding a plausible alternative with personal investment gives an appeal even greater credibility.
4. **Help the person understand the consequences of his or her decision.** Judah points out that taking Benjamin will have grave ramifications for his father.

Is there a situation in which you feel an injustice has been done that you would like to address? If so, how can you apply one or more of these principles from Judah's speech in your situation?

Judah has undergone quite a change since we first met him in Joseph's story. Let's look at how he has changed over time.

Read each passage and write in the blank the letter of the corresponding event described below.

_____ 37:26-27   _____ 38:15-16   _____ 43:9   _____ 44:33

Judah's Storyline in Genesis

A. Judah solicits a prostitute who he later learns is his daughter-in-law.
B. Judah suggests they sell Joseph instead of kill him so they won't have guilty consciences.
C. Judah takes the lead in offering up his life for Benjamin's in a speech to Joseph.
D. Judah personally guarantees Benjamin's safety to his father.

How do you see Judah changing and growing as the story progresses?

While Judah has come a long way and has emerged as a leader, his story isn't flawless.

Reread Genesis 44:27-28. How do you think hearing Judah recount this part of his story made Joseph feel?

It is as if Judah and the brothers have told this lie so often that their fiction has become fact in their minds. They have a story, and they are sticking to it. This scenario helps us remember that in the testing of his brothers, Joseph isn't looking for perfection. He sees both their faults and their definite change. And what he's interested in is their change.

The brothers got rid of Joseph years earlier, and they now have a golden opportunity to leave their dad's new favorite behind—but they don't take it. One authority comments, "To their credit they do not at this moment abandon Benjamin,…and head for Canaan as quickly as possible with their new supplies. Instead they choose to return to Egypt. The brothers' solidarity with their vulnerable, young, guilty brother will not be overlooked by Joseph."[20]

I do wonder if Joseph felt a hint of jealousy upon realizing that his brothers were willing to defend Benjamin though they maliciously sold him. He was human and surely had such thoughts and emotions, as we all do. But based on his willingness to reveal his identity (as we soon will see), I believe that overall he must have been pleased with the change he saw in them.

As we ride our own roller coasters of forgiveness and reconciliation, we might be tempted to look for one flaw or mistake to excuse not taking off our own masks and reconnecting. We need to remember that we are all sinners. Just today I let something slip out of my mouth that I instantly regretted. Can you relate? This message about grace ministers to us so much because we are so in need of it. If our friends and family waited to share their hearts and lives with us until we had it all together, we sure would be lonely, wouldn't we?

Ultimately what Joseph is looking for is safety. He knows that some people aren't safe. Clearly his brothers weren't safe on the day that they listened to him pleading from the bottom of a cistern. So it would be unwise for him to trust them again without testing to see if they have changed and it is safe for him to risk revealing himself to them. With a wife and two little boys, he has a lot at stake.

As you consider rebuilding trust with someone who has hurt you in the past, what are some ways you can test to see if it is emotionally, spiritually, and physically safe to proceed?

What qualities, characteristics, or habits make a person unsafe—and thus make it unwise for you to attempt reconciliation?

Certainly we need the guidance of the Holy Spirit to know when and how to determine safety and how to interpret our perceptions. Even though there still is a lie woven into Judah's story, Joseph must detect true repentance and change in his brothers. One author writes, "Only by recreating something of the original situation—the brothers are again in control of the life and death of a son of Rachel—can Yosef be sure that they have changed. Once the brothers pass the test, life and covenant can then continue."[21]

It's important for us to remember that there is a difference between forgiveness and trust. God always calls us to forgive, but He does not always call us to trust—or to reconcile. Trust can be lost quickly, but it is earned slowly. Scripture provides many examples of when trusting isn't a good idea. Here are just a couple:

- Jacob left home because his brother Esau planned to murder him. He could not trust him—just as Esau could not trust the brother who had betrayed him. (Genesis 27)
- Jonathan tested Saul's anger toward David and realized David wasn't safe in the palace. David fled and lived in caves until it was safe. (1 Samuel 20)

Of course, we want to be careful not to give up on relationships without intentional evaluation, testing, and confirmation; this is why we need God's clear guidance when it comes to making decisions about whether to trust those who have hurt or betrayed us. Though I pray that the decision to trust will be the rule rather than the exception, there are some cases when it is simply inappropriate to trust—times when trusting would expose us and others in our care to physical, mental, emotional, or spiritual harm. And we should not feel guilty for our lack of trust in such instances.

I have a dear friend whose stepfather sexually abused her in her childhood. The family swept it under the rug and couldn't understand why she wouldn't bring her children to holiday and family events when she became an adult. She felt strongly about not having her children around a man who had done these things with no consequences or repentance. Others in the family criticized her decision as unchristian and accused her of unforgiveness, but she knew God was calling her to keep her distance. She chooses to forgive her stepfather in her heart, but she does not trust him or want to have her children interacting with him. His refusal to repent prohibits them from reconciling. Her choice continues to cause difficulty in her extended family relationships today, but after much prayer she senses that God continues to confirm her decision to withhold trust.

I once had a relationship in which I could no longer open myself up because the person continually twisted my words and repeated a new version to others. This person also had a pattern of excusing these offenses rather than owning and apologizing for them. While it wasn't a matter of physical safety, the mental anguish from these actions being repeated over the course of years took its toll. Pebbles thrown over and over at the same spot can cause damage. If offenses are repeated without repentance, we may need to forgive and then move out of harm's way until the day that repentance opens the door for reconciliation.

Remember, forgiveness and reconciliation are not one and the same. For reconciliation to occur, there must be repentance on the part of the offending party.

Jesus told his disciples in Matthew 10:16, "Look, I am sending you out as sheep among wolves. So be as shrewd as snakes and harmless as doves." Joseph wrestled with grace, but he also exercised shrewd judgment in watching his brothers and determining God's perfect timing to reveal his true identity and test his brothers' repentance.

Lewis Smedes says that there are two obstacles to reconciliation, and both forgiveness and repentance are required to remove these obstacles. He writes:

> When a person close to us wrongs us, he throws up two obstacles between us. One of the obstacles is our sense of having been violated, which produces our anger, our hostility, our resentment. This is the obstacle that our forgiving removes. But only the person who wronged us can remove the other obstacle. And he can remove it only by repentance and, if need be, by restitution.[22]

Joseph chose forgiveness, but he needed to determine if repentance on the part of his brothers would allow them to reconcile.

How about you? Have you ever realized that you needed to distance yourself either physically or emotionally from someone you could no longer trust? If so, what were the circumstances?

Did a time ever come when you were able to reconcile? Why or why not?

It can be heartbreaking when we find we can't trust someone we have forgiven. Even through the loneliness of a lost relationship, the hopeful truth is that we can always trust God.

Read John 14:1 in the margin. Why does God tell us not to let our hearts be troubled?

"Don't let your hearts be troubled. Trust in God, and trust also in me."

(John 14:1)

Read Through Joseph's Family Story:

Read Genesis 35.

We can always put our trust in our loving Father. We never need to question whether He has our best interests at heart! He always does. Even when we find that someone we love is not safe for us to fully reveal ourselves to, we can always get real with the God of the universe. We never need to wear a mask with Him.

Talk with God

Spend some time now thanking God that He is trustworthy and all sufficient in your life. He is El Shaddai, God Almighty. Ask Him to give you clear guidance about whether He would have you pursue reconciliation in any strained or broken relationship. While we can't hurry the process and get ahead of God, we always should be asking, "Is there anything You would call me to do to make this difficult relationship better?"

Sometimes God asks me to call, text, or meet with someone to attempt to repair a relationship, and other times He whispers the familiar line from the theme song to the movie *Frozen*: "Let it go." I pray you hear Him loud and clear for His calling in your life today.

Day 5: Getting off the Ride

Marilyn's roller coaster ride took a new turn when she received a call from her senior pastor saying that her husband had died unexpectedly. Her husband, who was only forty-eight years old, had been out on a bicycle ride when he suffered a medical emergency that caused him to fall from his bike. Naturally she was scared and sad as she and her three children mourned their loss and faced so much uncertainty.

Looking back, she sees God's hand of mercy in bringing them to a new church home that cared for them through their grieving and continues to be a support to them. She remembers sweet times that her husband had with each child in the weeks and months prior to his death. She has hope because she has seen God's faithfulness over and over on the roller coaster ride of life, especially through the incidents with her father and former church. For Marilyn, the need to continually keep a soft heart through every trial remains an exercise in faith.

One day when she reentered the building of her former church where she and her husband had previously served, she felt some old hurts resurface. She scheduled an appointment with her current pastor to discuss her emotional response to being in that building. She wondered if her pain meant she hadn't fully forgiven. He assured her that pain isn't a sign of unforgiveness. Though we can forgive and even reconcile, it doesn't mean we forget. The ups and downs of forgiveness

Pain isn't a sign of unforgiveness. Though we can forgive and even reconcile, it doesn't mean we forget.

and reconciliation continue as long as we tread this earth. For this reason, we must always focus on Christ's love and grace toward us so that we can continue to extend it to others.

As we conclude our study of Genesis 43 and 44 this week, let's explore some related passages that teach us about God's heart for reconciliation. Throughout the Old and New Testaments, God is the great Reconciler. From the first sin, we see God pursuing a restored relationship with His fallen people.

One of my favorite stories involves an unnamed woman who made an appeal in Judah-like fashion to King David.

Read this woman's words from 2 Samuel 14:14 in the margin and write a short summary of what she is trying to communicate about God:

"All of us must die eventually. Our lives are like water spilled out on the ground, which cannot be gathered up again. But God does not just sweep life away; instead, he devises ways to bring us back when we have been separated from him."

2 Samuel 14:14

God pursues us relentlessly. He devises ways to bring us back when we have gone astray.

As you think about your walk with Christ, what are some ways He has pursued you?

God desires a close relationship with us—His people. He didn't even spare His own Son to bridge the gap of sin.

Read Colossians 1:19-23 and answer the following questions:

What were we like before God reconciled us? (v. 21)

How did God reconcile us to Himself? (v. 22a)

How does He see us now? (v. 22b)

God reconciles us to Himself through Christ. He asks only that we accept His offer of restitution for the sin that separates us from Him.

According to John 1:12 in the margin, what is our part in the reconciliation process?

> But to all who believed him and accepted him, he gave the right to become children of God.
>
> (John 1:12)

When did you believe and accept God's gift of salvation through Christ?

In the space below, write a prayer of thanks for God's provision of His Son so that we could be reconciled to Him.

Forgiveness is a nonnegotiable for all Christ-followers. You might say that we are called to be professional forgivers. God modeled this for us by sending His own Son to die in our place. C. S. Lewis wrote, "To be a Christian means to forgive the inexcusable, because God forgave the inexcusable in you."[24] God calls us to forgive but doesn't leave us without His power to do it. Like a glove that moves only with a living hand inside, God's Spirit moves our forgiveness fingers as we yield to Him. The process of reconciliation, however, isn't fully dependent on our choice or actions. As we've seen, it takes at least two to reconcile. This is what distinguishes reconciliation from forgiveness. They are sisters but not twins. Lewis Smedes clarifies it well in his book *The Art of Forgiveness*:

> "To be a Christian means to forgive the inexcusable, because God forgave the inexcusable in you."
> —C. S. Lewis

It takes one person to forgive.
It takes two to be reunited.

Forgiving happens inside the wounded person.
Reunion happens in a relationship between people.

We can forgive a person who never says he is sorry.
We cannot be truly reunited unless he is honestly sorry.

> We can forgive even if we do not trust the person who wronged us once not to wrong again.
> Reunion can happen only if we can trust the person who wronged us once not to wrong us again.

Forgiving has no strings attached.
Reunion has several strings attached.[25]

How can you apply these truths in your life personally?

The Scriptures have much to say about reconciliation or peacemaking.

Read the following verses and circle any words that relate to peace or reconciliation:

23 "So if you are presenting a sacrifice at the altar in the Temple and you suddenly remember that someone has something against you, 24 leave your sacrifice there at the altar. Go and be reconciled to that person. Then come and offer your sacrifice to God."

(Matthew 5:23-24)

If it is possible, as far as it depends on you, live at peace with everyone.

(Romans 12:18 NIV)

18 And all of this is a gift from God, who brought us back to himself through Christ. And God has given us this task of reconciling people to him. 19 For God was in Christ, reconciling the world to himself, no longer counting people's sins against them. And he gave us this wonderful message of reconciliation.

(2 Corinthians 5:18-19)

13 Make allowance for each other's faults, and forgive anyone who offends you. Remember, the Lord forgave you, so you must forgive others. 14 Above all, clothe yourselves with love, which binds us all together in perfect harmony. 15 And let the peace that comes from Christ rule in your hearts. For as members of one body you are called to live in peace. And always be thankful.

(Colossians 3:13-15)

List below some instructions from these verses related to forgiveness and reconciliation:

Joseph forgave, and he pursued reconciliation as well. He did it carefully, slowly, and, I believe, very prayerfully. Let's review the events that have unfolded in Joseph's story this week and consider the relevant truths we can apply in our own lives.

As you read, circle two truths (right column) that especially echo into your current circumstances.

Joseph's Story	Relevant Truths
Jacob withholds sending Benjamin to Egypt.	We must be careful not to hold on too tightly to things out of fear.
Judah speaks truth to his father about the need to release Benjamin into his care to save the whole family.	We must speak truth in the face of others' unrealistic expectations, blaming, and paralyzed grief.
Jacob ultimately resigns himself to trust El Shaddai and releases his beloved son to Judah's care.	Even if we get to the point of cynical resignation, when we release what we've been holding on to, we can trust our All-Sufficient El Shaddai.
Joseph breaks down with emotion and has to leave the room when meets his long-lost brother Benjamin.	Sometimes we can be overcome with emotion during the reconciliation process. It's okay to run away and have a good cry.
Joseph's brothers leave Egypt and set out for Canaan thinking everything turned out fine.	Sometimes when we think a relationship seems fine, God might want to take us deeper through testing and trial to reveal our character.
A silver goblet is found in the favored son's sack and all of his brothers return with him to face charges and stand behind him.	Brothers who once tried to kill the favored son can change and get over their sibling rivalry and become supportive even if Dad picks a new favorite. People CAN change.
Judah becomes a leader and gives a speech appealing to Joseph and offering his life in exchange for Benjamin's.	A person who struggled with self-control like Judah (selling Joseph, soliciting a prostitute) can emerge as a leader when they yield to God's way. Even if we have serious sin in our past, God can use us in mighty ways.

Describe how the two truths you circled speak to you and your circumstances:

Behind the scenes of what seemed like a roller coaster of ups and downs, God was working out a reconciliation plan for Joseph's family. One writer observes that "the faith, penitence, tender emotions, and loyalty that unite a family are now being fashioned."[26]

God wants to help us on our own roller coasters of forgiveness and reconciliation, especially when we feel like closing our eyes, tightening our grip, and just enduring the ups and downs. We don't always understand the scenarios that play out in our stories, but we can trust El Shaddai to be all sufficient and use every twist and turn.

The difficult part for me comes when I'm unsure whether to let my guard down and pursue honest conversation in an attempt to reconcile, or whether to wait and pray until the other party is ready. I desperately want to reconcile relationships when hurt has occurred, especially when I know I contributed to the problem because of my sin. I want to fix it and make it right. Yet sometimes others are simply unwilling. If we have repented and sought peace and others do not want to reunite, we must resign ourselves to leave uncomfortable situations alone. We can pursue peace only as much as it depends on us. Then we must leave the rest in God's hands.

We leave the narrative with a cliffhanger this week. Jacob waits at home, wondering what will become of his family. Benjamin faces a jail sentence. Judah hopes his offer to sacrifice himself for his brother will be accepted. The other brothers aren't sure what will happen next. Joseph hasn't yet revealed his true identity. The story is unresolved at this point, just like many of the relational situations in which we find ourselves. Yet God is always at work in hearts and minds even when everything seems in limbo in our relationships. Just as He was at work in the midst of the complications between Joseph and his brothers, so He gives us hope for our fractured relationships.

Next week we will continue Joseph's reconciliation encounter. We also will explore the role of setting boundaries and finding a new normal as relationships begin to heal. Whether you are experiencing a relationship high or low right now, I pray God will work miracles and use you to build bridges of reconciliation.

Read Through Joseph's Family Story:

Read Genesis 36.

Talk with God

Think of something in your life that remains in limbo—unresolved. Ask God to give you clear direction about whether you are to take any action steps toward reconciliation or to leave it alone. Spend some time listening to Him right now.

In Psalm 32:8, the Lord says, "I will guide you along the best pathway for your life. / I will advise you and watch over you." You can rest in obeying Him, knowing that He will guide you on the best pathway for reconciliation—whether it is making a phone call, addressing issues in person, reconnecting in some way, or releasing the situation to God and trusting in His plan and timing.

Digging Deeper

What was it like for Joseph to transition from life in Canaan to life in Egypt? What were the cultural differences? Does the biblical account correspond with archaeological and historical data? Check out the Digging Deeper article for Week 4, "Walk Like an Egyptian," to find some parallels in your life as a follower of Christ living in an often hostile environment (see AbingdonPress.com/Joseph).

VIDEO VIEWER GUIDE: WEEK 4

The Roller Coaster Ride

I planted the seed in your hearts, and Apollos watered it, but it was _____ who made it _____. It's not important who does the planting, or who does the watering. What's important is that God makes the seed grow. (1 Corinthians 3:6-7)

The tyranny of pain:

We naturally _____ hurt, and it can lead to the _____ of our soul.

_____ at living in peace with everyone, and work at living a holy life, for those who are not holy will not see the Lord. Look after each other so that none of you fails to receive the grace of God. Watch out that no poisonous root of _____ grows up to trouble you, corrupting many. (Hebrews 12:14-15)

The human spirit can endure a sick body,

> *but who can bear a _____ spirit? (Proverbs 18:14)*

In the midst of the tyranny of pain, God has given us a token of _____.

We desperately want someone to _____ _____ for us when we're in pain.

Isaiah 53:3-6 – Jesus stood up for us.

Psalm 34:18 – The Lord is close to the brokenhearted.

He will not crush the weakest reed
> *or put out a flickering candle.*
> *He will bring justice to all who have been wronged. (Isaiah 42:3)*

Week 5

GRACE AND BOUNDARIES

Genesis 45–46

Memory Verse

Don't repay evil for evil. Don't retaliate with insults when people insult you. Instead, pay them back with a blessing. That is what God has called you to do, and he will bless you for it.

(1 Peter 3:9)

Day 1: Come Closer

"Words cannot fully describe the pain and loss I felt." These words from Matthew West's book *Forgiveness* are shared by Renee, who tells the story of losing her twenty-year-old daughter, Meagan, when a drunk driver caused a traffic accident. Describing her struggle to forgive the man who caused the death of one of her twin daughters, she says: "For a long time I'd thought that by forgiving…I would be betraying my daughter." At his sentencing, the young man turned and spoke to the family, weeping and saying he was sorry. This helped Renee find a moment of healing in her life. She reflects, "Suddenly, instead of anger, I began to feel compassion for this young man who had made a tragic mistake." Renee later appealed for a sentence reduction in an act of grace toward a person whose decisions had caused great pain and loss in her life.[2]

To go from the point of pain to the place of extending grace toward those who wound us is truly a supernatural act that takes testing, time, and truth. This week we reach a climax in the Genesis narrative with a big reveal on Joseph's part. We left the story last week with a cliffhanger after Joseph tested his brothers with a silver cup found in Benjamin's sack. Judah then gave a humble speech on his little brother's behalf. In his commentary on Genesis, Bruce Waltke writes, "Judah's speech proves beyond doubt that the formerly hateful, selfish brothers are now motivated by love for one another and have integrity within themselves and with one another."[3]

Joseph has tested the men who had thrown him into a pit and sold him into slavery two decades earlier, and now he finds it safe to stop the charade and take off his Egyptian mask.

Read Genesis 45:1-8. Underline every statement Joseph directs toward his brothers. Circle the sentences describing the responses of his brothers.

[1] Joseph could stand it no longer. There were many people in the room, and he said to his attendants, "Out, all of you!" So he was alone with his brothers when he told them who he was. [2] Then he broke down and wept. He wept so loudly the Egyptians could hear him, and word of it quickly carried to Pharaoh's palace.

"The Egyptian wisdom literature prized a 'cool,' controlled spirit. Now Egypt's wisest man gives expression to a higher wisdom of authentic passion."[1]

³ *"I am Joseph!" he said to his brothers. "Is my father still alive?" But his brothers were speechless! They were stunned to realize that Joseph was standing there in front of them.* ⁴ *"Please, come closer," he said to them. So they came closer. And he said again, "I am Joseph, your brother, whom you sold into slavery in Egypt.* ⁵ *But don't be upset, and don't be angry with yourselves for selling me to this place. It was God who sent me here ahead of you to preserve your lives.* ⁶ *This famine that has ravaged the land for two years will last five more years, and there will be neither plowing nor harvesting.* ⁷ *God has sent me ahead of you to keep you and your families alive and to preserve many survivors.* ⁸ *So it was God who sent me here, not you! And he is the one who made me an adviser to Pharaoh—the manager of his entire palace and the governor of all Egypt."*

What responses, reactions, or phrases stand out to you from Joseph's unveiling? How do Joseph's brothers respond?

Imagine for a minute the awkward moment after Benjamin has been caught with a silver cup and Judah has made a humble appeal, offering himself in his brother's place. Given their experiences with this unpredictable Egyptian official, the brothers certainly aren't expecting him to dismiss his attendants and cry uncontrollably in front of them. Two other times Joseph had gone into another room to cry (Genesis 42:24 and 43:30), but this time he isn't running to pull himself together. He allows himself to appear vulnerable.

I can think of times when I have wanted to get words out but the tears choked me so that it took several minutes before I could utter an explanation. It's good to be reminded that we aren't the only ones who struggle to hold it together emotionally, right?

Can you think of the last time you had a good, hard cry that made communication difficult? If so, briefly describe it below.

For me, this often happens at the most inopportune times when I desperately don't want to cry (the doctor's office, in front of a group of people, at my child's school, and so forth). I remember the day I went into the school counselor's office to inform them of my daughter's alopecia and to request a note that would give her permission to wear a hat to school until we could find a hairpiece. It was a simple request that I knew they would grant. Yet I got so choked up just uttering the words that I could barely speak.

Unbidden waterworks can erupt when we try to give a voice to the reality of our pain. I'm sure if Joseph could have chosen, he would have preferred to speak without the overwhelming emotion that was heard by everyone outside the doors. Either those doors were thin or he was a loud crier!

Joseph is one of the rare biblical characters of whom very little is said about his flaws. We mainly see his trust in God, his ability to forgive, and his love for his family. Here we at least get a glimpse of his humanity. God made us emotional beings. Big girls do cry—a lot! Strong emotions often accompany situations in which we are dealing with pain from our past, reconciliation in the present, or boundaries for the future.

Look back at Genesis 45:3 (page 134). What was the first statement Joseph made to his brothers once his attendants left the room?

Now review the words used to describe the reaction of Joseph's brothers in Genesis 45:3 (page 134). If you have access to a searchable online Bible, look up this verse in several different translations and note below any different words that are used to describe their reaction.

I can only imagine the mixture of disbelief, concern for their lives, clarity about past interactions, guilt, and many other things that could have been rolling around in their heads in this moment. They can't even wrap their minds around the fact that their brother is not only alive but his dreams of having authority over them have been realized. While they are reeling in shock, Joseph speaks again. His words provide a great model for us in the reconciling conversations we have with those who have hurt us, identifying four important concepts.

1. Request Any Needed Affirmations

The first thing Joseph asks concerns the welfare of his father: "Is my father still alive?" (Genesis 45:3). He already knows his father is still alive, having asked this same question previously (Genesis 43:27-28). It's as though he is saying, "Please tell me again." When coming to a moment of truth, affirmations are often needed.

One time my husband, Sean, saw a friend in the church parking lot after the worship service and felt there was awkwardness between them. Although they had not had a conflict, Sean and this man's very close friend were reconciling after an argument. Sean said, "Are we okay?" He looked at Sean and said, "Yes, we are fine. It's like two of my friends had a fight on the playground and made up. We are good." My husband simply needed affirmation that their friendship wasn't affected.

Doubt and worry can cause us to feel insecure throughout the reconciliation process, so we need to be willing to boldly ask for affirmation even if we've already been told once that things are okay.

When have you needed to ask someone to affirm what you thought was true in a relationship—just to be sure?

2. Communicate "Come Closer"

The next thing Joseph says is, "Please, come closer" (Genesis 45:4). Joseph has observed his brothers and now feels safe to invite them to come closer—physically and emotionally. Remember that he has tested the waters first. We don't invite alligators to come close. But once we have patiently, slowly, and carefully tested our offender, we need to follow Joseph's example and use words and body language that communicate the message, "Come closer."

Notice the tactics Joseph doesn't use—the things he doesn't say or do. He doesn't

- rehash the specifics of his pain.
- make punitive remarks.
- give shame.
- exude bitterness or hardness.
- make passive-aggressive jabs.

I admit there have been times when I have wanted to reconcile with my husband after exchanging harsh words, but I have wrongfully used some of these negative tactics. Even when we want to make things better, it can be tempting to throw in a little shame here or a jab there. Unfortunately, it fails to communicate, "Come closer." In fact, it sometimes can be like pouring gasoline on a flame, which ends up making the situation worse instead of better.

We would do well to learn from Joseph's wise example of reconciliation dialogue. He grappled with grace privately until he was ready to extend it

publicly. After an argument, it is better for us to wait to approach the other party until God has fully worked truth and grace into our hearts, so that the words that overflow clearly communicate, "Come closer."

Think through a past reconciliation. How did you communicate the message "come closer" to someone? What words, body language, or actions did you use?

In a current fragile relationship that you feel is safe to repair, what is one practical way that you can communicate, "Come closer"?

3. Acknowledge the Truth

Though Joseph says, "Come closer," he also states the truth of the matter. "I am Joseph, your brother, whom you sold into slavery in Egypt" (Genesis 45:4)—these are the next words he speaks after asking them to come near. Joseph isn't heaping on guilt here, but neither is he sugarcoating. He is not only clarifying his identity but also communicating that from here on out, the fictitious story they have been sticking to for a long time must be replaced with truth. He wants them to come closer, but he seems to know that it won't be possible without honest admission of the wrong that was done.

Lewis Smedes says this about the importance of truthfulness:

> Without truthfulness, your reunion is humbug, your coming together is false. With truthfulness, you can make an honest new beginning....To be specific, you must expect those who hurt you to be honestly in touch with the reality of your falling-out, your pain, and their responsibility for them.[4]

I have tried to reconcile without truthfulness, but I have learned that once a falling-out has caused distance, trying to come closer by sweeping it all under the rug merely maintains a façade. We can avoid the painful past and attempt to pretend nothing happened, but we can't truly come closer with that elephant always in the room. The reality is that something happened, and all parties must recognize the event and the pain that it caused.

In Joseph's case, the hurtful event was one-sided. His brothers wronged him. Sometimes we are the perpetrator, and other times we are the victim.

Often we are both. When reconciling, usually both parties have some things they can own that they aren't proud of or would do differently in hindsight. Maybe you started the fracture with hurtful words, but then the other person gossiped to someone about it. Perhaps another person lied about you, but then you reacted with angry words. In his book *Forgive and Forget*, Smedes lists four things that are necessary for truth when reconciling with others who have hurt us:

- They must truly understand the reality of what they did to hurt you.
- They must be truthful with the feelings you have felt.
- They must be truthful in listening to you.
- They ought to be truthful about your future together.[5]

Just as we expect this from our offender, so we must be willing to take this posture in order for true reconciliation to occur. Of course, we can't expect our understanding of what happened to perfectly align with theirs. Smedes explains it this way:

> No two people in the history of personal misunderstandings have ever remembered their painful experience in the same colors and the same sequences, because no two people have experienced the same hurt in precisely the same way. So, if you want total recall, blow for blow, insult for insult, hurt for hurt, you will never get what you need.[6]

Because we will never see things in exactly the same light as others, we need the bare minimum of acknowledgment of feelings and truth concerning the basic circumstances.

Joseph had heard his brothers' account of what they did to him on their first visit to Egypt (Genesis 42:21), and he does not take the opportunity to correct them now. This moment of reconciliation is not a long rehash of the details but a simple statement of the truth of what they had done to hurt him: they had sold him.

It is important to note that perception and truth are not always the same thing. Truth consists of irrefutable facts.

Look at the statements below and mark T for truth (an undeniable action) and P for perceptions (someone's interpretation of what happened):

_____ You raised your voice above its normal tone.

_____ You threw something across the room.

_____ You were late to something that is important to me.

_____ You served me with divorce papers.

_____ You put me in a pit and sold me into slavery

_____ You directed that general comment on social media at me.

_____ You intentionally ignored me at the party.

_____ You intended to hurt me by not inviting me.

_____ You judged my parenting by not allowing your child to come to my house.

_____ You like other people more than me.

The first five statements are truth (T), and the last five are perceptions (P). Perceptions involve judging motives or deciding what others are thinking or feeling. Though they may feel like reality to us, they may or may not reflect the truth. Trying to align our perceptions with those of others often leads to deeper hurt. We cannot play detective, using clues from our own perspective to make assumptions about what others are thinking and feeling. Communication is paramount to sorting through perceptions.

On the other hand, truth—undeniable actions that wound us or others—must be acknowledged in order to move forward in reconciliation. Showing up late, throwing something, hanging up the phone, raising your voice, lying, and other undeniable actions must be admitted and acknowledged if we are to repair a relationship.

Choose one of the following questions and write a brief response:

1. When have you tried to reconnect with someone but found you couldn't move forward because the other person was unwilling to acknowledge the pain he or she had caused through words or actions?

2. When have you tried to reconnect with someone but found it only got worse as you rehashed the situation and your differing perceptions continually collided, making the situation worse?

When others feel hurt because they perceive that we ignored them, slighted them, or failed to include them, we must be willing to acknowledge their pain even though our motive was not to harm. We must communicate in order to sort through motives, and we must believe one another rather than try to determine one another's thoughts or feelings based on perceptions alone.

Joseph not only speaks the truth; as he does so, he also makes God the focus of his words of reconciliation.

4. Focus on God

Immediately after speaking the truth, Joseph follows it with these words: "But don't be upset, and don't be angry with yourselves for selling me to this place" (Genesis 45:5). There is no penitence necessary; it is already forgiven. Joseph doesn't play the victim card. Instead he chooses to view the barbaric treatment he has endured as something God is using as a lifesaver for many. Joseph doesn't talk much about himself here. As Warren Weirsbe notes, "It wasn't a time for explanations and excuses but for honest expression of love and forgiveness."[7]

Unfailing love and truth have met together.

Righteousness and peace have kissed!

(Psalm 85:10)

Read Psalm 85:10 in the margin. Write below the two things that have met together and kissed:

_____   _____

Joseph truthfully says that his brothers sold him into slavery, but his words are flavored with loving mercy and grace. His focus is on God, not himself. He looks to that second story that God is building, saying, "It was God who sent me here" (Genesis 45: 5), rather than using accusing words. Joseph sees God's redemptive power even in his brothers' past cruel behavior.

Can you put the focus on God and see something beneficial that has come from harm caused by others? If so, describe it below:

How might focusing on God's redemptive power help you to "come closer" to that person or those persons in reconciliation?

There have been times when I have desperately wanted to "come closer" in a strained relationship, but we couldn't move forward because there was not an acknowledgment of feelings and facts between us—much less a focus on God's redemptive power. It's hard to let go of the habit of reading into the actions, motives, and feelings of others, especially when social media "creeping" is so prevalent.

We can look at a few pictures and statements and find ourselves determining in our minds another person's level of happiness or feelings toward us. When pursuing reconciliation with someone, sometimes one of the best ways we can "come closer" is simply to stay off of each other's social media feeds. Without added distractions, it is easier to communicate and keep our focus on God as we view the situation through His eyes.

God wants reconciliation, but just as we need to acknowledge the truth of sin in order to draw closer and reconcile with God, so we must acknowledge the truth of hurtful words and actions in order to "come closer" and reunite with others. Distance remains—whether physical or emotional or both—between those who are "never wrong" and just want to move on, pretending nothing ever happened. Keeping our focus on God, remembering His great mercy and grace and power to redeem, can help us to have the perspective we need in order to have effective reconciling conversations with others.

> *The journey to forgiveness rarely ever comes without time, testing, and wrestling with the truth.*

Review the four things we can learn from Joseph's reconciliation speech in Genesis 45, and rewrite them below in your own words:

1.

2.

3.

4.

Reading someone else's story of forgiveness and reconciliation can make the journey seem easier than it is. As we all know from experience, the journey to forgiveness rarely ever comes without time, testing, and wrestling with the truth. And like Joseph, we are not able to complete it on our own. Tomorrow we will focus even more intently on the supernatural element of forgiveness as God helps us have His gracious eyes to see others and our situation, all the while depending on Him.

Talk with God

Take some time to thank God today that He sent His only Son so that we can come close to Him. Acknowledge the truth that we fall short of

His holy standards all the time. Then praise Him for his amazing grace that forgives and erases all our sin: "I—yes, I alone—will blot out your sins for my own sake / and will never think of them again" (Isaiah 43:25).

Ask God to help you follow His example by forgiving someone in your life today. Specifically, ask Him to help you request any needed reaffirmation, communicate "come closer," discern and acknowledge the truth, and focus more on Him than anyone or anything else.

Day 2: Talking Freely

Forgiveness stories affect us so deeply because we know their power. It's difficult to forgive. We struggle to forgive everyday occurrences such as the family member who irritates us, the husband or child or coworker who takes us for granted, and the friend who gossips about us. So when we hear more challenging forgiveness stories such as Renee's account of forgiving the drunk driver who killed her daughter (yesterday's lesson), or Louis Zamperini's tale of extending grace to the cruel prison guard from a Japanese POW camp (Week 2), or Joseph's story of pursuing reconciliation with his brothers who betrayed him, we are keenly reminded that forgiveness and reconciliation are possible. Joseph's story causes us to say to ourselves, "How did he do that? I want to do that. I want to be free and forgive others as I have been forgiven by God."

Celestin Musekura's journey to forgiveness falls in the ranks of "against all odds" forgiveness stories. While he was studying at a seminary in Kenya in 1994, his home country of Rwanda saw nearly one million people killed in a period of one hundred days. Among those killed were his family and members of the church where he had served as pastor for three years in a village in Rwanda. He then committed his life and ministry to helping people in the aftermath as they worked toward community practices for making peace. His book *Forgiving As We've Been Forgiven*, written alongside Duke University professor L. Gregory Jones, gives great insight into his journey to forgiveness.

As we will see today in the reconciliation between Joseph and his brothers, forgiveness is much more than one moment affecting only the parties involved. The scope of forgiveness is farther and wider than we could ever comprehend. Like pebbles thrown into calm waters, the ripples of both relational fracture and healing extend far beyond the original point of impact. So before we return to the Genesis account, let's use a wide-angle lens and zoom out to see the bigger picture of forgiveness.

Turn to Matthew 6:9-15. Read this model prayer, and make notes below of anything that strikes you about forgiveness:

Look back at verses 11 and 12. What are we to ask for before asking for forgiveness?

Fun Fact:
Genesis 45 is the center of the Joseph account recorded in Genesis 37–50.

When was the last time you went a day without food? In the same way, receiving and extending forgiveness isn't a one-time thing. It's *daily*. Forgiveness lives at the center of the gospel of Christ. While we sometimes focus on our daily need for it, we often forget the daily practice of extending it. Celestin Musekura, the Rwandan pastor whose story I shared earlier, notes, "Just like food, forgiveness sustains our lives in the community. Just as we cannot live without daily bread, we cannot fully live our life in communion with each other and with God without the ability to grant and receive forgiveness."[8]

Receiving and extending forgiveness isn't a one-time thing. It's daily.

How does identifying forgiveness—both receiving and extending it—as a daily need (such as food) encourage or discourage you in your current pursuit to forgive?

As we read about great men and women like Renee and Celestin Musekura and Joseph, who forgave and blessed their persecutors, we must remember that it is a daily journey. One scholar points out, "We must assume that Joseph perceived bit by bit the hand of God in this nightmare."[9] As I reflect on my own internal struggles with forgiveness, it helps me to remember that Joseph's story, recorded in just thirteen chapters, spanned a lifetime. Though a cursory read may make Joseph's forgiveness toward his brothers and his focus on God's plan seem quick and uncomplicated, it was likely a daily practice—much as it is for you and me.

Now, turn to Genesis 45:9-15 and read Joseph's next instructions to his brothers for moving forward. Write three words or phrases to note the speed at which Joseph wants all of this to happen:

1. Verse 9a:

2. Verse 9b:

3. Verse 13:

Though Joseph took his time in revealing himself to his brothers, now that he has done it, he is anxious to enact plans so that he may see his beloved father. One of the blessings of forgiving and reconciling with others is that it can open the door to relationships that sin had nailed shut—not only those immediately involved but also those of mutual friends, extended family members, and acquaintances. Whether it's a physical or emotional barrier keeping the door shut, reconciliation can knock the rusted hinges off a door that has been impassable for decades.

Have you ever found that reconciling with someone has positively impacted other mutual relationships? How did this bring a blessing in your life?

When and how have you encountered the peripheral effects of unforgiveness? This is when others can't get along, and it brings discomfort and alienation for those around them.

When we work things out with family, friends, coworkers, neighbors, or church members, it lessens the strain on others caught in the crossfire. For Joseph, forgiveness not only meant reuniting with his brothers but also gaining access to a man he dearly loved and missed: his father.

A secular radio show host asked listeners this question: "Have you ever held a grudge and why?" People called in and told their stories. It was crazy to hear about a mother and daughter who didn't speak for five years because the daughter forgot to come by after work and help her with taxes. Another woman said she hadn't talked to her brother in thirty-one years after a dispute over an inheritance. She wore it like a badge of honor. I thought of the other relatives involved and the difficulty and strain they must have experienced at weddings, funerals, and other family events. Forgiveness and reconciliation free us to communicate with and bring blessing to those on the bordering edges of a conflict.

Reread Genesis 45:14. Joseph is weeping again, but what is the reason given this time for his tears (see NLT)?

Joseph took a huge risk in revealing himself, and now he finds joy gained through opening up and showing his true self. Until now, there has been no touching or dialogue.

Take a look at Genesis 45:15. What do the brothers do after Joseph kisses and weeps over each of them?

As Warren Wiersbe observes, "'Afterward his brothers talked with him' (Gen. 45:15 NIV) is a simple sentence that speaks volumes in what it doesn't report."[10] I like the wording of the New Living Translation, which says "they began talking freely with him." Once again we see that Joseph doesn't shame, punish, or even make passive-aggressive references to his brothers. But we also can note some things that his brothers do not do. Here we do not find any:

- Excuses
- Interruptions
- Explanations
- Corrections of details

How could any of the above have hindered their ability to reconcile with their brother?

Can you recall a time when any of these behaviors hindered your ability to reconcile with someone? If so, describe it briefly below:

Though moments earlier the brothers were so shocked that they didn't respond at all, now they are talking freely—and without offering excuses or explanations. We find a different interaction here than in their previous exchanges with Joseph in Egypt or those of the early years.

Turn to Genesis 37:4 and recall the brothers' communication with Joseph when he was a teenager. Describe it below:

After the harsh words of the early years, the many years of silence, and then the guarded and sometimes inauthentic communication they had

when Joseph's identity was masked, this conversation briefly referenced in Genesis 45:15 is a whole new concept for the brothers. Joseph knows his brothers look back with regret; he heard them talking about it on their first trip to Egypt. So although we do not get many details here, we can assume apologies were offered as they talked.

I like the fact that the text is silent about the exact words that were spoken between the brothers, because I believe there are no forgiveness formulas—though I have found that when you are the offender, as I have been many times, fewer words tend to be better than more: "I did it, and I'm sorry. I recognize that it was wrong and that it hurt you." Rather than giving us forgiveness formulas, God gives us principles that lead us into His presence, where we must rely on Him for supernatural help both to ask for and to extend forgiveness. As I've read many books on the topic, I've found myself turned off by the ones purporting to follow some rigid outline when it comes to forgiveness. Hurt is messy, and grace is messier. It requires an individual wrestling with God and then relying on His help.

Recall a time when you were able to talk freely again with someone after a conflict. What helped you get from conflict to open communication in your situation? (There is no right answer. We can learn from one another as we hear the types of things that help us put feet to the forgiveness and reconciliation process.)

> Rather than giving us forgiveness formulas, God gives us principles that lead us into His presence, where we must rely on Him for supernatural help.

I think of a silly argument my husband and I had recently. We went from innocent conversation to offense in lightning speed. We misunderstood each other and made accusations and excuses. You might say we did the opposite of everything we see in today's passage. Until we worked it out, we couldn't talk freely. If we had had to talk about where the kids needed to go or something involving our home or calendar, it would have been evident to every fly on the wall that we weren't "talking freely."

What impact does an unresolved offense with someone close to you tend to have in your communication?

Whether the conflict is a little spat or a major betrayal or wound, forgiveness is necessary in order to get to the point of reconciliation where we can talk freely. Celestin Musekura found himself training pastors one year after his family had been killed. Among the group he discovered three pastors who were related to the men responsible for the attack on his village. Anger and resentment began to cloud his view until God called him to repent. He writes, "I had allowed my pain, grief, anger, and bitterness to eclipse my spiritual eyes. But the Lord showed me the reality of my shared identity with these brothers in Christ. We all belonged to the family of Christ. Our shared identity in Christ was superior to any other identity that culture, tradition, and history had assigned to us."[11]

Beginning to see others as children of God helps us develop "spiritual eyes," as Musekura mentions. With God's help we can get to the point where, like Joseph, we can weep for joy, show our affection, and talk freely even with those who have caused us great pain.

> Think about someone who has hurt you. Now, take a minute to write below how God sees this person:

> *Beginning to see others as children of God helps us develop "spiritual eyes."*

Continuing to keep this person in mind, read a few verses in which God says how He feels about His children:

But you, O Lord,
*   are a God of compassion and mercy,*
slow to get angry
*   and filled with unfailing love and faithfulness. (Psalm 86:15)*

"This is my commandment: Love each other in the same way I have loved you." (John 15:12)

But God showed his great love for us by sending Christ to die for us while we were still sinners. (Romans 5:8)

Notice the progression of these verses.

- God is full of mercy and compassion and slow to get angry with us.
- God commands us to love others in this same way.
- God loved us so much that He sent His only Son to die for us.

As you think about the person who irritates you, has deeply wounded you, or has said or done something in between those two extremes, ask God to help you imitate Him in loving this person. As we begin to pray daily for forgiveness and recognize that we need it like food, we will find

God supernaturally enabling us to offer His grace to others. Then, as He gives us His spiritual eyes, we can view others as He does—as children of God, our brothers and sisters in need of love.

If Celestin Musekura could forgive the people who killed his family and Joseph could reconcile with his brothers who set out to harm him and sold him into slavery, do you believe it's possible for you to forgive and perhaps even begin to talk freely with people who have hurt you?

____ No, I'm still not convinced that it is actually possible for me to forgive what has been done to me.

____ Yes, I believe it's possible to forgive, but I'm still wrestling with God right now.

____ Yes, I believe it's possible to forgive, and I am asking for God's help.

If you checked the last blank, can you think of any bold moves God may be calling you to take in order to get to the point of open and loving communication with an offender in your life?

Talk with God

Spend some time in God's presence right now, asking Him if there is any alienation in your life He is preparing you to end through dialogue. Wait on His timing. Don't get ahead of Him, but don't lag behind Him either.

As you strive for open communication with this person or persons, ask God to reveal any inhibitors that might be preventing reconciliation. Is there anything from today's text in Genesis 45 that you can practically apply?

Check any that you hear His Spirit prompting a need for attention.

____ Taking a risk by initiating contact
____ Letting your guard down and revealing your true self
____ Recounting a situation without shaming or punishing.
____ Listening to your offenses without getting defensive or making excuses
____ Considering the ripple effect of a conflict
____ Asking daily for forgiveness and the ability to extend it

Allow God to reveal any action steps or prayer items, and then spend some time thanking Him for His supernatural ability to heal the greatest of offenses in our lives.

Meditate on this passage as you conclude your time talking with God: "Do not judge others, and you will not be judged. Do not condemn others, or it will all come back against you. Forgive others, and you will be forgiven" (Luke 6:37).

Fun Fact:

Joseph was thirty-nine years old when he was reunited with his father, Jacob.[12]

Day 3: Unleashing Grace

There is a beautiful story in Corrie Ten Boom's book *The Hiding Place* that illustrates for us the power of God in us as we submit to His command to forgive:

> It was at a church service in Munich that I saw him, the former S.S. man who had stood guard at the shower room door in the processing center at Ravensbruck. He was the first of our actual jailers that I had seen since that time. And suddenly it was all there—the roomful of mocking men, the heaps of clothing, Betsie's pain-blanched face.
>
> He came up to me as the church was emptying, beaming and bowing. "How grateful I am for your message, Fraulein," he said. "To think that, as you say, He has washed my sins away!"
>
> His hand was thrust out to shake mine. And I, who had preached so often to the people in Bloemendaal the need to forgive, kept my hand at my side.
>
> Even as the angry, vengeful thoughts boiled through me, I saw the sin of them. Jesus Christ had died for this man; was I going to ask for more? Lord Jesus, I prayed, forgive me and help me to forgive him.
>
> I tried to smile, I struggled to raise my hand. I could not. I felt nothing, not the slightest spark of warmth or charity. And so again I breathed a silent prayer. Jesus, I cannot forgive him. Give Your forgiveness.
>
> As I took his hand the most incredible thing happened. From my shoulder along my arm and through my hand a current seemed to pass from me to him, while into my heart sprang a love for this stranger that almost overwhelmed me.
>
> And so I discovered that it is not on our forgiveness any more than on our goodness that the world's healing hinges, but on His. When He tells us to love our enemies, He gives, along with the command, the love itself.[13]

Corrie Ten Boom ended up starting a rehabilitation center for those affected by the war. She even reached out to those who had cooperated with the Nazis, realizing that they also needed God's love and grace.

Today as we return to Joseph's story of reconciliation in Genesis 45, we will find Joseph going a step beyond forgiveness, unleashing grace toward his brothers.

Read Genesis 45:16-26. In the left column, list everything that Pharaoh suggests Joseph give his brothers. In the right column, list the items Joseph gives them.

Items Pharaoh Suggests   Items Joseph Gives

Note that Joseph is still a man under authority. Even though God has blessed him and exalted him from his place of humility, he still answers to Pharaoh. Pharaoh outdoes Joseph by extending his offer of the best land and the choicest food, as well as giving consideration to the family's wives and children with the suggestion of carts or wagons.

Let's look specifically at two of the items Joseph sent with his brothers and consider their relevance in other parts of the story. Read each verse and summarize who is involved and what they are doing with the particular item:

Clothing	Silver
Genesis 37:23	Genesis 37:28
Genesis 45:22	Genesis 45:22

What contrast do you see between the ways that each item is used?

Joseph had been stripped of his robe, but here he provides his brothers with clothes. One scholar points out that in Scripture, a change of clothes often signals a new beginning, and this certainly is a new beginning for Joseph's brothers.[14]

While the brothers took twenty pieces of silver for their evil deed of selling their brother, Joseph generously gives Benjamin fifteen times that amount.[15] Even Joseph's previous act of slipping money into his brothers' bags can be viewed in a positive light. Whether that was pure generosity or a way to test them in order to establish trust, we see him using shekels with good intentions.

Joseph went beyond forgiving to actually *blessing*. In the New Testament we see this concept of blessing those who persecute us expounded even further.

Read 1 Peter 3:9 in the margin. What does God say He will do to us if we will give a blessing to those who have hurt us?

> *Don't repay evil for evil. Don't retaliate with insults when people insult you. Instead, pay them back with a blessing. That is what God has called you to do, and he will grant you his blessing.*
>
> *(1 Peter 3:9)*

Now look up Romans 12:14-21 and complete the following summary statements:

_____ those who persecute you; don't _____. them. (v. 14)

Never pay back evil with _____. (v. 17)

Since God will do it for you, don't take _____. (v. 19)

Don't let evil conquer you, but instead _____. (v. 21)

Which one of these commands really hits home with you right now? Why?

The word *never* in verse 17 is convicting to me. We can't make any exceptions here. God calls us to bless our enemies, and He will empower us just as He did for Corrie Ten Boom when she faced her prison guard. God calls us to go above and beyond the bare minimum in these verses.

Just as Joseph couldn't muster up forgiveness in his own strength, we too must believe that if we will take the first steps in obedience to these clear commands, even when we don't feel like it, God will enable us through His mighty power to accomplish it.

How do we bring our feelings in line with God's truth found in Romans 12? Henry Cloud says that "feelings should neither be ignored or placed in charge."[16] We can't discount our very real emotions, but we also can't allow them to rule since they are so fickle. Following God must supersede following feelings. It's easier said than done. At times I have asked God to help me release a hurt, yet my feelings seem pokey about coming around. Every new little offense seems to reignite those old emotions. I can be like an army trooper patrolling the demilitarized zone after a truce, looking for an infraction in my marriage, friendships, or other relationships. Intellectually I know God calls me to forgive, but I'm just not "feeling it." Can you relate?

Can you recall a situation—past or present—when you were battling emotionally between wanting to hold on to hurt or seek retribution and knowing you should forgive? If so, describe it below:

Nancy Leigh DeMoss tackles the problem of what to do when we want to forgive but can't move forward in her book *Choosing Forgiveness*. She writes:

> I've talked with people who believe they've truly forgiven their offender—they've pressed the delete key—but they still feel stuck emotionally. When they think of that person, they still feel tied up in knots....God's Word gives us an important key to going all the way with forgiveness. It requires that we go "above and beyond" just releasing our offender—that we extend the grace of God and build bridges of love by returning blessings for cursing, good for evil.[17]

So, when we want to choose forgiveness but struggle against our feelings, we can set out to intentionally bless our offender. Instead of letting our thoughts and feelings run wild, we can turn our focus to pursuing creative ways to give a blessing.

Perhaps there is someone you have been struggling to forgive—someone who is a "relational enemy" right now. You want to move on, but you find the hurt this person has caused creeping into your daily thoughts.

Jesus said, "But to you who are willing to listen, I say, love your enemies! Do good to those who hate you. Bless those who curse you. Pray for those who hurt you" (Luke 6:27-28). Are we willing to listen? What could we do to bless those who have hurt us?

Here are a few ideas:

- Bring a meal to someone who neglected you in a time of need.
- Write a note of encouragement to someone who usually has only criticism for you.
- Leave a little gift on the porch of someone who has pulled away from you.
- Purposely speak well of someone who has spoken ill of you.

Let these ideas be a springboard to get your creative juices flowing!

What could you do to bless someone who is a relational enemy right now? Ask God to give you direction for a tangible idea:

> *Bless those who persecute you. Don't curse them; pray that God will bless them.*
>
> *(Romans 12:14)*
>
> *"But to you who are willing to listen, I say, love your enemies! Do good to those who hate you. Bless those who curse you. Pray for those who hurt you."*
>
> *(Luke 6:27-28)*

Wouldn't it be great if we could combine all of our ideas and create a Pinterest board of ways to bless those who have hurt us!

Of course, there are times when we must keep boundaries with the person we need to forgive—such as ex-husbands, abusers, and unrepentant people who continue to wound. In such cases we should exercise caution in choosing a blessing that won't reopen an unhealthy relationship. Nevertheless, there is always at least one way we can bless even these people.

Read Romans 12:14 and Luke 6:27-28 in the margin. How do these verses suggest we bless those who curse us?

It's impossible to continue in bitterness with a hard heart when you continually pray blessings on someone.

Both of these passages mention praying for those who persecute or hurt us. Our loving Father knows that it's impossible to continue in bitterness with a hard heart when you continually pray blessings on someone. It softens us and blesses them. Corrie Ten Boom felt God doing a supernatural work in her heart as she cried out to Him for help in forgiving the guard who had so mistreated her. He will do the same for us. As we pray for others and for the ability to forgive, God works His forgiving miracle of healing in our hearts that we cannot accomplish apart from Him.

Joseph is a good example for us when it comes to doing the hard work of moving beyond feelings to forgiveness. He not only forgave, he blessed his family with material goods and assured them of his care for them. He set their minds at ease and lived out his changed heart toward them. I'm sure this was as much of a daily pursuit as sitting down for meals. Yet Joseph persevered in forgiveness. He applied God's truth to his pain and chose to bless his brothers. We, too, can make choices contrary to our negative feelings by praying and looking for ways to bless those who have hurt us.

Talk with God

Thank God that He not only forgives you but also chooses to bless you. We can unleash grace only as a conduit of what we've received from Him. Bask in His amazing grace for a few moments.

Now spend some time praying for those who have "persecuted" or hurt you. Ask God to bless them and to show you appropriate ways that you may bless them too.

Day 4: Boundary Lines

I've wrestled through setting boundaries in relationships very personally in the past few years. I found myself struggling with two sins that God revealed in my heart, mind, and mouth. Exclusivity and gossip had gone unchecked and had grown in my life. My sin grieved the heart of God, and He called me to repent. In order to fully obey Him, I needed to draw boundaries in some relationships. It was tough and lonely, and it caused pain in the lives of some people I dearly love. Yet it was clear that boundaries were necessary in order to be obedient to God and turn away from sin in my life.

Boundaries are something we must set carefully and prayerfully. Sometimes we can put up a baby gate with just a few limitations in a relationship only to find that a stone wall has been erected on the other side of our gate in retribution for our boundaries.

As Joseph unleashed grace onto his brothers, he had a healthy sense of boundaries. Boundaries can be a difficult part of our messy forgiveness stories. After reconciling, we often struggle to find a "new normal" in an old relationship. We have seen God work through our confessions, repentance, and reunion, bringing healing where once there was hurt. Now the questions become, *Where do we go from here? How can we interact in a healthy way without falling into old, destructive patterns?*

As we pick up with Joseph's story, I wonder, *How will the brothers keep from falling back into jealousy over the favor that Jacob is bound to give Joseph? How close will Joseph and his brothers become now that they have reconciled?* Forgiveness plus grace is not a recipe for naivety. Joseph knows what his brothers are like.

Turn to Genesis 45:24, and write below the instructions Joseph gives his brothers:

Joseph certainly knows his brothers well. Being all too familiar with their bent for deceitfulness and disagreement, he urges them not to argue on their way home. One scholar observes, "The text literally says, 'Don't get excited.' The brothers are not to make recriminations against one another regarding their crime, especially in explaining it to their father. If Joseph forgives them, how much more should they forgive one another."[19]

Reconciliation doesn't mean Joseph never advises, warns, or instructs his brothers. He actually sets a limit on how they are to treat one another. Joseph apparently knows the truth of Psalm 133:1: "How wonderful and pleasant it is / when brothers live together in harmony!"

As a boy, Joseph would have seen boundaries modeled in his father's relationships with his father-in-law, Laban, and his twin brother, Esau. Jacob and Laban had a complicated relationship from the beginning. Laban had deceived Jacob by giving him Leah for a wife instead of Rachel after Jacob had worked for seven years to marry Rachel. Later, God blessed Jacob's flocks more than Laban's, causing Jacob's wealth to grow and exceed that of his father-in-law.

What does Genesis 31:1-3 say began to happen in Laban's attitude toward Jacob?

Describe a relationship in your life that, through time and circumstances, changed as the other person's attitude toward you changed.

What did the Lord tell Jacob to do in verse 3?

Sometimes God calls us away from difficult relationships, and other times He asks to stay engaged and fight to make it better. Laban pursued Jacob after he heard the news of his departure. There were accusations, defensiveness, and threats in their dialogue, unlike the dialogue when Joseph and his brothers came together. Finally Laban and Jacob made a covenant.

According to Genesis 31:51-55, what were the terms of the covenant?

The New Living Translation uses the word *boundary* in verse 53: "So Jacob took an oath before the fearsome God of his father, Isaac, to respect the boundary line." Henry Cloud writes, "Boundaries define us. They define *what is me* and *what is not me*. A boundary shows me where I end and someone else begins, leading me to a sense of ownership."[20] With a clear boundary in place, we don't feel responsible for managing the life and emotions of others; instead, we are able to seek God for His direction in tending our own spiritual yards. We are always called to forgive those who trespass against us, but that doesn't mean we can't put up a fence so that the access to do it again is limited.

What boundaries has God asked you to put in place for emotional or physical health in a complicated relationship? (Perhaps it is the relationship described above with someone whose attitude toward you began to change.)

Jacob also had a toxic relationship with his twin brother, Esau. As we learned earlier in our study, Jacob fled his childhood home after Esau threatened to murder him for stealing the birthright and blessing. In Genesis 32, after Jacob leaves Laban with a boundary line, he must head through his brother's territory. It is here where Jacob wrestles with God.

How have you wrestled with God over a boundary line in a relationship?

In Genesis 33, we find that Jacob and Esau have a peaceful encounter where they kiss and hug, much like Joseph and his brothers. However, what happens according to verses 14-20?

This account fascinates me. After their emotional moment of reconciliation, Jacob turns in the opposite direction. In verse 20 it says, "And there he built an altar and named it El-Elohe-Israel." Jacob's name had been changed to Israel in Chapter 32 after his wrestling match with God at Peniel; so when he calls the altar "El-Elohe-Israel," he is naming it "God of Israel"—in other words, "the God of me." Jacob likely hurts Esau by not following him and reestablishing an ongoing relationship with him. Boundaries are often perceived as hurtful. They are a rejection of sorts.

As much as God loves reconciliation, He also recognizes a time for boundaries of protection. As we seek God, we will find His direction on when to put up emotional, spiritual, or physical walls for safety and when to tear them down. Just as He is the God of Israel, so He is the God of me and you—showing us when to pursue intimacy and when to turn around and head in the other direction.

We desperately need the help of God's Spirit coupled with wisdom from His Word to know how to navigate a new normal in a reconciled relationship.

- How much of our secrets will we reveal?
- What amount of time and emotional energy will we invest?
- We may let someone into our lives, but should we let her or him into our soul?
- Are there some lines we need to draw regarding what we won't do or allow?

We can learn about setting boundaries from recovering addicts, who often draw strict lines about being in environments where they will be tempted or associating with those who engage in their old behavior. Perhaps this is why the Serenity Prayer, which is all about boundaries, is so prevalent in twelve-step programs.

In addition to setting a limit on how his brothers were to treat one another, we see Joseph setting a couple of other boundaries in Genesis 45.

Review Genesis 45. In what ways do you see Joseph subtly drawing boundaries in his brand new relationship with his brothers?

If we always allow others' emergencies to become ours, we can neglect the work God has called us to do.

I noticed that Joseph isn't moving his brothers into his home. Instead they will settle in the land of Goshen, a region outside the city where Joseph lives, with land for tending livestock. Goshen is near Joseph (Genesis 45:10) but not in his backyard. It also is interesting that Joseph doesn't accompany them on their journey back to Shechem to retrieve their father and families. Instead, he continues to do his job as an administrator overseeing famine relief. Joseph provides what they need for their journey but stays on task, doing the work God has called him to do. There's an important lesson here for us: if we always allow others' emergencies to become ours, we can neglect the work God has called us to do. Does that speak to anyone other than me?

Often I feel pulled between tasks that God has called me to do and people who have needs. Sometimes in my effort to help others, I overinvolve myself and prevent them from walking the path God has for them. At times God does call us to drop a task to bear another's burden, but in other situations He cautions us not to insert ourselves too heavily in someone else's journey. When we do for others what God has called them to do for themselves, we can unintentionally harm instead of help.

As you continue to wrestle with the boundary lines in your relationships, remember that you don't have to go it alone.

Write your name in the blank:

God is El-Elohe of _____.

God will help you, lead you, and wrestle with you through the speed bumps in your relationships.

God is the God of you. God will help you, lead you, and wrestle with you through the speed bumps in your relationships. As we end today, give some thought to all that God has revealed to you about boundaries in relationships—both through His Word and through His Spirit.

Summarize in one sentence what God has revealed to you through His Word about boundaries in relationships:

Read Through Joseph's Family Story:

Read Genesis 41.

Has God given you clarity through His Holy Spirit about any current or needed boundary lines in your own relationships? If so, write what you have heard from Him below:

If not, keep seeking and knocking. God is faithful to direct us. He is the God of you and also El Shaddai—the All-Sufficient One in your life. Claim Proverbs 3:5-6: "Trust in the LORD with all your heart; / do not depend on your own understanding. / Seek His will in all you do, / and he will show you which path to take."

Talk with God

Reinhold Niebuhr, a great theologian-philosopher, is said to have penned the words to a prayer in preparation for a church service in Heath, Massachusetts, more than eighty years ago. In 1944, a portion of the prayer was published and distributed to the armed forces and then later adopted by Alcoholics Anonymous. Known as the Serenity Prayer, it has helped many people seeking clarification and direction in setting boundaries. Let's end our day offering the best-known version of this heartfelt prayer to the Lord. Though the words may be familiar, pray with fresh eyes and a sincere heart:

> God grant me the serenity
> to accept the things I cannot change;
> courage to change the things I can;
> and wisdom to know the difference.[22]
> —Reinhold Niebuhr

Day 5: Moving On

After living in Canada for the first three years of marriage, Sean and I moved to Ohio with our one-year-old son. We left behind an amazing church family and friends that we still love and cherish eighteen years later. In Canada, my husband's family had been nearby, and now we would be living in a city with no relatives anywhere near us. However, I'd be lying if I said I wasn't excited to move back to the States, leaving behind the six months of Canadian winter, snow and ice, the long distance from my Texas family and friends, colored money—well, you get the idea. Leaving our familiar surroundings and friends made the move bittersweet, though, giving us a mixture of emotions on our new adventure.

Recall a move you have made, whether across town or across the country. What were some difficult things as well as things you looked forward to about a fresh start?

Fun Fact:

"The land of Goshen was located in the northeast part of the Nile delta, an area of about nine hundred square miles, very fertile and excellent for grazing cattle."[21]

Jacob was 130 years old when he made the journey from Canaan to Egypt, and he lived seventeen more years in Egypt (Genesis 47:9, 28).

Today we will read about a major move for Joseph's father, Jacob, and his family. Jacob finally had released Benjamin to travel with his brothers to Egypt when the famine gave him no other choice. Now he waits anxiously at home, hoping and praying for a safe return of his sons. He trusts in El Shaddai, the All-Sufficient God—and I imagine him checking the horizon daily for signs of the travelers' return.

Read Genesis 45:25-28 and record Jacob's first and second reactions to the news of his son Joseph being alive.

1.

2.

What does Jacob say that he wants to do?

At first Jacob's response is stunned disbelief, but when he hears all that Joseph said and sees all that he sent, he accepts the news and seems excited to go visit his long-lost son. Jacob exclaims, "It is enough" (Genesis 45:28 NKJV, RSV). Though on one level he is saying that all he has heard and seen is enough to convince him that Joseph is alive, he also is expressing his satisfaction in the news. Jacob is finding sufficiency in El Shaddai, the All-Sufficient One.

Jacob's declaration that he will go and see his son before he dies seems to imply that he hasn't fully embraced the idea that this reunion will require a fairly permanent move away from the land God had promised to his family—away from home and familiarity. He had struggled with fear to release Benjamin. Now he must release all he has known and cherished to adapt to a new land full of different customs, and at his age this has to be tough for him.

Elderly people tend to have the reputation of disliking change and finding comfort and security in familiarity. And the older I get, the more I understand the concept of people becoming set in their ways. I like my familiar cup with my preferred brand of tea, and I find myself settling into all sorts of other little particular routines beyond my teacup. If I put myself in Jacob's shoes, I can understand how unsettling it might have been to think about leaving his home for good.

Read Genesis 46:1-7 and note below the first thing Jacob does when he arrives at the first stop on his journey, Beersheba:

Jacob has been living in the land of Hebron, but Beersheba is the land of his youth where he deceived his brother Esau (Genesis 25:28-34; 27:1-46). He stops here on his journey to make a sacrifice to the Lord. One commentator observes, "A father on his way to see his son pauses to worship the God of his own father."[23] Isn't that beautiful? Jacob takes the time before a major life transition to ask for God's help and blessing.

As we enter into new phases of life such as becoming a mother, parenting teens, starting a new job, or moving to a new community, we can learn from Jacob's example the importance of taking some time out from the craziness that usually surrounds these transitions to focus on God. When we find ourselves at a crossroads, it is wise to stop and worship God as Jacob did—to reflect on God's provision and grace and seek His guidance.

For Jacob, who lived under the Old Testament law and worshiped God through the system of animal sacrifices (which was a shadow pointing to Jesus; see Hebrews 10:1-19), this was no quick or unplanned act. Offering a sacrifice…

When we find ourselves at a crossroads, . . . it is wise to reflect on God's provision and grace and seek His guidance.

- was intentional.
- took preparation and time.
- required resources or cost.

As I've reflected on Jacob's dedication, I've thought about how we could be more intentional about worshiping God during some of the crossroads moments and big moves in our own lives. The list of ways we could dedicate new phases of life to the Lord is endless, but here are just a few ideas:

- Take a day to fast, focusing on God and listening to Him (the fast could be from food, social media, or anything that God might identify).
- Have a family prayer over a new home, dedicating it to God.
- Pray together as a family in the car as you prepare for a long road trip.
- Choose a particular book or section of the Bible to read and study during a transition in life (e.g., illness: the Book of Job; moving: Abraham's story; wedding: Song of Solomon).

What other ideas can you add to the list?

Because one of life's constants is change, we would do well to use times of adjustment or transition as opportunities to worship and draw near to God.

After Jacob makes a sacrifice to God, we find a rare occurrence in the Old Testament called a theophany. This is an appearance of God Himself.

What does God say to Jacob in Genesis 46:3-4?

Why do you think Jacob needs to hear these assurances?

Much like you and me, Jacob struggles with fear. We've already seen that he had feared losing Benjamin. Commentators point out that he also might have been thinking of the prophecy God gave to his father, Abraham, about his descendants being slaves for four hundred years in a foreign land (Genesis 15:13-16). In any case, God wants to calm his anxiety.

Did you know that the command used most frequently in all of Scripture is not "be good" or "love others" but "fear not"? I think God knows us so well and is keenly aware of how often we are scared out of our minds—especially when we encounter change.

What fear is currently on your radar?

I sometimes fear that my daughter with alopecia will never have her hair grow back, or that my son will have disappointments at the college he chose. I also can feel my heart thump out of my chest when I know I'm going to be addressing a delicate issue in a relationship that could cause conflict. Other times my fears are completely irrational. I won't even give examples because they seem too silly to write.

Whatever our fears may be, our gracious God wants to calm them. He doesn't shame us for having them. Instead, He says to us the very same words He spoke to Jacob, telling us not to be afraid of whatever new transition is on the horizon because He will go with us. The Lord spoke these same words to Joshua in Deuteronomy 31:8: "Do not be afraid or discouraged, for the LORD will personally go ahead of you. He will be with you; he will neither fail you nor abandon you." The writer of Hebrews recalls these words in the New Testament:

For God has said,

"I will never fail you.
*   I will never abandon you." (Hebrews 13:5b)*

God promises never to leave us. When I left my small hometown in Texas to attend college in downtown Chicago, I had some anxiety. I remember God whispering to me that I wouldn't be alone, assuring me that He has a home office up north, too! Life is a journey full of risks, fears, and what-ifs, but we are never alone.

How does the promise of God's constant presence encourage you in your current fears?

Getting back to Genesis 46, we find in verses 8-26 a list of the people who traveled from Hebron to Egypt. Although this is one of those lists that typically we might skim over, these names represent real people that God loved and pursued.

After the record of those on the journey, we get to the big moment where Joseph and his father reunite.

Read Genesis 46:28-34 and note their reactions below:

Joseph (v. 29)	Jacob (v. 30)

There is much weeping and little talking on Joseph's part. By forgiving and reconciling with his brothers, Joseph regains the father he had lost many years ago. He spent his first seventeen years with his father, and now he will have another seventeen years with him in Egypt before Jacob dies at the age of 147. Joseph also gains the blessing of having his entire family with him—his brothers and many nieces and nephews.

Reconciling with people who have hurt us can open the door for blessings in other relationships. When we refuse to forgive or reconcile with our offenders, we can miss out on collateral relationships along the way. For example, when we leave a church over a problem with the pastor or one individual, we can miss the sweet fellowship of others. Or when we can't reconcile with one friend, we can lose our relationships with mutual friends caught in the crossfire. But as we forgive and reconcile, we experience blessings that also affect others around us.

Now as we finish Genesis 46, we find Joseph instructing his family on what they are to say to Pharaoh.

Read Genesis 46:33-34. Why does Joseph warn them to tell Pharaoh that they are shepherds?

Verse 34 tells us that, knowing they are shepherds, Pharaoh will allow them to live in the land of Goshen, because the Egyptians despise shepherds. I wonder if Joseph is protecting them in some way. Perhaps he knows his family will be left alone or won't be seen as a threat to Egyptian commerce. Or perhaps he is protecting them from the temptation to intermarry with the Egyptians or adopt pagan practices, which God had clearly warned his people not to do. Another option is that Joseph just wants them to be totally honest with Pharaoh. He knows his brothers have a history of deceit, and perhaps he wants to be sure they don't tarnish his reputation as a man of integrity in Egypt.

No matter the reasons behind Joseph's instructions, we see him reuniting and caring for the welfare of his family. As they move into a new land that Joseph has known for over two decades now, he leads, provides, and reconnects with his family. It is a beautiful picture of God's amazing grace.

As we end our week of study on grace and boundaries, let's do a quick review.

Read the themes we have discussed throughout the week, and circle the one that resonates most strongly with you:

1. *Come Closer*: Joseph revealed himself and asked his brothers to come closer. He acknowledged the truth about the harm they had done in his life, but he also made God the focus of the conversation.
2. *Talking Freely*: Joseph set his brothers at ease and wept over them. They came to a point of talking freely. On this day we looked at the Lord's Prayer and found forgiveness to be a daily need in our lives just as our need for food.

3. *Unleashing Grace*: Joseph blessed his brothers with new clothes and gave Benjamin a large amount of silver. Though his brothers had taken his robe and sold him into slavery, he didn't repay evil for evil but instead showed generosity and love.
4. *Boundary Lines*: Joseph saw his own father draw boundary lines with his father-in-law and his twin brother. Joseph set boundaries with his brothers by not residing in Goshen with them and by making his new job a priority rather than traveling with them.
5. *Moving On*: We saw Jacob encounter God on his way to see Joseph. God reminded him not to be afraid because He would not leave him, even in the pagan land of Egypt.

Why does the theme you circled resonate with you right now?

Read Through Joseph's Family Story:

Read Genesis 42–43.

Talk with God

Spend some time in God's presence, asking Him if there is anything He is calling you to do in a relationship in order to

- come closer
- talk freely
- unleash grace by giving a blessing to someone who has offended you
- draw a boundary line of protection
- move on to a new situation with a focus on God

Listen for His voice and ask for clarity and confirmation of what you hear Him calling you to do. Praise and thank Him for being "the God of you." He invites us to come closer and talk freely; He longs to bless us; and He promises never to leave us. Write a prayer of thanksgiving in the space below that focuses on these character traits of God.

Digging Deeper

We need to forgive others, but can we forgive ourselves? Joseph's brothers thought God might be punishing them for what they did to their brother even two decades later. How can we break the chains of our past and walk in the freedom God gives us through Christ? Check out the Digging Deeper article for Week 5, "Forgiving Ourselves: Breaking the Chains of Our Past" (see AbingdonPress.com/Joseph).

Grace and Boundaries

Whether we are the offended or the offender, it's always our _____ to make peace.

God blesses those who work for peace,

for they will be called the children of God. (Matthew 5:9)

But the wisdom from above is first of all pure. It is also peace loving, gentle at all times, and willing to yield to others. It is full of mercy and the fruit of good deeds. It shows no favoritism and is always sincere. And those who are peacemakers will plant seeds of peace and reap a harvest of righteousness. (James 3:17-18)

God calls us one step further, and that is not to just make peace but then to also offer a

_____.

Finally, all of you should be of one mind. Sympathize with each other. Love each other as brothers and sisters. Be tenderhearted, and keep a humble attitude. Don't repay evil for evil. Don't retaliate with insults when people insult you. Instead, pay them back with a blessing. That is what God has called you to do, and he will grant you his blessing. (1 Peter 3:8-9)

VIDEO VIEWER GUIDE: WEEK 5

Sometimes in the aftermath of pain, we have to maintain some

_____.

3 Types of Boundaries

1. _____ invisible boundary

   A few things are off limits in the relationship.

2. _____ boundary, like a fence

   Reunited but not totally intertwined.

3. A _____, or complete barrier

   When others will not admit what they've done and there is no repentance,

   sometimes physical presence is unsafe or unwise.

Joseph had boundaries. But the way he navigated them was he kept his _____

on _____ through the process.

God has sent me ahead of you to keep you and your families alive and to preserve many survivors. So it was God who sent me here, not you! And he is the one who made me an adviser to Pharaoh—the manager of his entire palace and the governor of all Egypt. (Genesis 45:7-8)

Week 6

MOVING FORWARD

Genesis 47–50

"You intended to harm me, but God intended it all for good. He brought me to this position so I could save the lives of many people."

(Genesis 50:20)

Day 1: Pilgrims

As I walked out the front door of my home one last time before leaving for college, I looked over at the porch swing. How many times had I sat there talking with Jesus? I worked at a day care center my last summer after graduating from high school, and the center gave me a two-hour lunch break every day because they didn't need as much coverage during naptime. It made for a longer workday, but I loved that time in the middle of the day. I often went home and sat on the porch with my Bible and my lunch, feeling God's nearness as I ate and read. Now as I headed to the car packed with all my stuff for college, I was excited and nervous at the same time about the new adventures I would have in Chicago. Pulling out of the driveway and beginning the seventeen-hour drive, I thought about sitting in the church sanctuary where I heard from God through the amazing sermons of my pastor and driving around in my car while singing along with Steve Camp. I wondered if I would sense God's Spirit in the same ways in new places. It's easy to associate a physical setting with spiritual moments.

How would my relationship with God change in a new church? Would I find private places to talk with Him on a busy college campus? I remember panic creeping up the back of my neck on the first day of Personal Evangelism class when the professor said that we would be required to share our faith with two different people that semester. Yet in that new classroom of strangers, I heard a familiar reassurance from God. My surroundings had changed, but He had not. He was going to see me through every step if I would walk closely with Him.

I remember that moment when I got married and moved to Canada and then later moved to Ohio. God reminded me that the scenery may change, but we're never alone on the journey of life.

As we reenter Joseph's story this week, we find that Jacob has departed the familiar land of Canaan to travel to a pagan land. Though Jacob has never been to Egypt before, his grandfather Abraham traveled there during a time of famine in his own life. In Egypt, Abraham lied to Pharaoh by telling him that Sarah was his sister rather than his wife (Genesis 12:10-20). Terrible plagues came upon Egypt as a result; so when Pharaoh discovered that Abraham

Fun Fact:

According to tradition, when Joseph went before Pharaoh, he "took with him Reuben, Simeon, Levi, Benjamin, and Issachar."[1] While some commentators think he took stronger brothers, rabbinic tradition believes he took weaker-looking brothers so that Pharaoh wouldn't be tempted to make soldiers out of them.

The scenery may change, but we're never alone on the journey of life.

and Sarah were married, he sent them away. Jacob's encounter with Pharaoh couldn't have been more different.

Read Genesis 47:1-12 and complete the chart below.

	Pharaoh's Question	Response
To brothers	(v. 3)	(vv. 3-4)
To Jacob	(v. 8)	(v. 9)

Joseph brings his brothers in first, having previously coached them about how to answer any questions about their occupation (Genesis 46:33-34). As an intuitive leader who knows Pharaoh well, Joseph wants his brothers to be honest about their livelihood as shepherds. Perhaps Joseph wants his family separated from the Egyptians so they will not be tempted by the pagan idolatry of the culture. One commentator notes: "Joseph emphasizes that his family are shepherds to assure Pharaoh that they entertain no social or political ambitions and to preserve them from an alien way of life and intermarriage with the Egyptians."[2] Pharaoh blesses them with the land of Goshen and even mentions the possibility of the brothers overseeing some of his royal sheep and cows.

Although we do not know for certain why the brothers and Jacob did not enter Pharaoh's presence at the same time, one scholar offers this suggestion: "Joseph delays in presenting his father to Pharaoh, possibly to avoid the embarrassment of having his esteemed father stand before Pharaoh to beg a favor, as did the brothers in v. 4."[3]

After Joseph presents Jacob before Pharaoh, the first topic of conversation is age. At 130 years old, Jacob is already twenty years past the average Egyptian age. Bruce Waltke notes that "Egyptians were preoccupied with death, and the pharaohs, who professed to be eternal, sought to immortalize their bodies."[4] Pharaoh is impressed by Jacob, not only because he is the father of Joseph, his second in command, but also because of his longevity.

Jacob's response to Pharaoh's question includes his status as a pilgrim or a sojourner. I like the New International Version that reads, "And Jacob said to Pharaoh, 'The years of my pilgrimage are a hundred and thirty. My years have been few and difficult, and they do not equal the years of the pilgrimage of my fathers.'" The Hebrew word for pilgrimage is *maguwr*, which is defined as "sojourning place, dwelling-place, sojourning, lifetime."[5] Warren Wiersbe writes, "Everybody has some metaphor to describe life—a battle, a race, a trap, a puzzle—and Jacob's metaphor was that of a pilgrimage."[6]

As you think about your life, how would you describe your pilgrimage? (Feel free to use one of the metaphors noted previously or come up with your own.)

None of our pilgrimages is exactly like that of another. The danger comes when we get stuck in the day and fail to see the larger picture of where we are headed. We easily forget that the road we are treading right now is temporary. Our true citizenship is in heaven. We are just visitors making a journey on this planet. We need to remember that we are pilgrims. Stuart Briscoe observes, "God's people through the ages have been encouraged to regard themselves as pilgrims and when they do they develop a unique approach to life."[7]

Read Hebrews 11:13 in the margin. What did the people referenced in this verse agree that they were?

All these people died still believing what God had promised them. They did not receive what was promised, but they saw it all from a distance and welcomed it. They agreed that they were foreigners and nomads here on earth.

(Hebrews 11:13)

When we realize that this earth is not all there is, it affects the way we view life. Briscoe asserts, "The pilgrim mentality is a must for the believer in all ages, not only for the weatherbeaten old timers like Jacob."[8]

At this point, Jacob knows that he has missed out on twenty-two years of Joseph's life because his sons sold Joseph into slavery. He could resent them so bitterly that it tears his family apart, yet he chooses a pilgrim mentality instead. A pilgrim mentality reminds us that life is short and that unforgiveness can keep us from those we love most—often the ones who seem to hurt us the most.

As you think about forgiving those who have offended you, how can the perspective that we are all pilgrims on a journey help you work toward reconciliation?

We miss the blessings of today when we are stuck in resentment for things that happened yesterday.

As we recognize that each one of us is on a journey, it gives us compassion for our fellow sojourners. They are "in process" just as we are. I have wasted time and mental energy on resentment over past hurts, which has spoiled my ability to enjoy the present journey alongside others. We miss the blessings of today when we are stuck in resentment for things that happened yesterday. God desires us to walk our roads together—especially in our families and the community of believers.

Jacob forgave his sons for selling Joseph into slavery. Think about that for a minute, imagining that they are your own children. If Jacob and Joseph could forgive, is there anything too big to be reconciled in your life?

Is there a person or situation that you need to release to God again today?

Now, take a moment and hold out your fist, open it, and lift it up, releasing this person or situation to God.

Turn to Genesis 47 and read verses 13-31. Does anything about Joseph's plan for the Egyptians seem harsh or unfair? If so, describe it below.

Though we have seen Joseph cry quite a few times in the Genesis account, he is no mushy, spineless man. In contrast, here we see the shrewd businessman that seems to be implementing a plan of enslavement.

What is the people's response to his plan according to verse 25?

The people are grateful for life. This concept may be hard to understand for those of us who have never known extreme hunger and loss. When people are stripped of everything, they often are willing to become dependent at any cost just to survive. This portion of the text helps give us perspective on the impact of a widespread famine. The people were gladly willing to sell themselves for grain. The severity of the famine highlights God's provision for Joseph's family in Goshen. As we consider the hunger and economic devastation happening throughout the land, we see God's mercy in bringing Jacob's family to Goshen to be well provided for by Joseph.

God uses a pagan nation as the place He chooses to prosper and multiply His people for this season of their journey. Later Moses will deliver them when their numbers become a threat to a new pharaoh. But for now Jacob and his sons have the opportunity to trust God as they live in a foreign land surrounded by famine, and God is taking care of them.

In Genesis we see God use a boat (Noah), a move (Abraham), a ram (Isaac), and a nation (Jacob and Joseph) to save His people from trouble. Nothing can stop God's commitment to us as we make our own pilgrimage through difficult circumstances. What we see as huge obstacles, God can use for our good. Our Lord works through divorces, deaths, illnesses, conflicts, and financial famines—that often seem insurmountable—when we encounter these speed bumps along our journeys.

> *What we see as huge obstacles, God can use for our good.*

In his later years, Jacob has the opportunity to realize that life often is more about the process than the physical places and circumstances in which we find ourselves. He seems to overcome his fear of releasing people to God and embrace El Shaddai, the All-Sufficient One, as his rescuer. Likewise, God wants us to let go of our fears and embrace Him as our All-Sufficient One in the midst of today's troubles.

Take a moment to pause and fix your mind on El Shaddai. Write a short prayer below, thanking Him that nothing can thwart His commitment to you:

Jacob makes one final request of Joseph in Genesis 47:29-30. What is it?

Jacob wanted his body taken back to Canaan where his father, Leah, and Rachel were buried. Joseph made a commitment to honor his father's last request. If we reflect on Jacob's pilgrimage, we see that he did have a hard life:

- His father-in-law tricked him into marrying Leah when he wanted Rachel.
- He had to put up with the feuding between his two wives and their two servants.
- His wife Rachel died in childbirth when Benjamin was born.
- His sons sold Joseph into slavery and lied about it.
- Famine forced him to expose his youngest son, Benjamin, to possible harm.
- He had to leave the home of his ancestors and travel to a foreign land in his old age.

Some of these things were out of his control, such as Rachel's death and the famine. Others were personal offenses requiring him to process hurt and hate in order to experience supernatural healing with God's help.

As you think about your pilgrimage—your journey through life—what experiences have been hard for you? List several.

1.

2.

3.

4.

Mine would include:

- Moving my junior year of high school to a new town.
- Finding out I was having twins ten days before I had them.
- Many health challenges for my children—some acute and serious and others slow and emotionally painful.
- Losing friendships.

As I reflect on the journey, I see God bringing good things out of the pain.

As you look over your list above, how can you see God's blessings even in the midst of a hard journey? Write your thoughts in the form of a prayer of praise to God:

Talk with God

Jacob could have thrown a fit about moving to a foreign land. He could have held a grudge against his sons for their many sins. Instead, he admitted that the journey was hard while realizing he was only a pilgrim in a much larger plan.

King David also acknowledged he was a sojourner on this planet, praying in Psalm 39:12:

Hear my prayer, O LORD!
  Listen to my cries for help!
  Don't ignore my tears.

For I am your guest—
    a traveler passing through,
        as my ancestors were before me.

Take a moment to pray this simple verse to God right now. If you are alone, pray it out loud. Ask God to give you His perspective on your own journey.

Day 2: Not What I Expected

Elizabeth found herself driving around town a lot, looking for her husband's car. As she wandered through apartment complex parking lots and different areas of town, she couldn't believe that things had come to this. After four years of marriage, her husband had informed her at her birthday dinner that he was having an affair and wanted to end the marriage. Now she wasn't even sure where he was. How had this happened?

As a follower of Christ, she never wanted to be divorced. Her college sweetheart didn't even want to try to work it out. She grieved and wondered *why*? Fresh tears filled her eyes as she recalled her dearly loved father asking what she had done to drive her husband away. He apologized later that day for asking such a question, but his words still stung like acid in a fresh wound.

As the years passed and she processed the pain and struggle of a broken relationship with the help of her loving God, she began to see that although divorce was not what she had anticipated, God had much to teach her through this unexpected occurrence along life's journey.

Today we find Jacob giving a blessing, but his actions and message are unexpected. They do not follow human logic and tradition. This is the first time in the biblical account that we see Joseph a little miffed about something. (Aren't you glad to know that he got upset sometimes too?)

Read Genesis 48:1-4 and write below the promises God made to Jacob back in Canaan:

Here Jacob again employs the name of El Shaddai, God Almighty, the All-Sufficient One. I believe that this truth that God is truly all sufficient for us and has our good in mind is the one our enemy most wants to attack with his lies and accusations. Satan wants us to see our temporary suffering as proof that God is not enough. Jacob reminds Joseph that Egypt is transitory and God will bring His people back to the land of Canaan. He repeats the

Fun Fact:
The well that Jacob promises to Joseph is the same well where "Jesus would meet the woman of Sychar . . . and lead her to saving faith (John 4:15)." [9]

promises of God to his son, and later Joseph will repeat God's promises to his brothers (Genesis 50:24).

God calls us to say His promises over and over again to ourselves and to those around us—especially the promise that He is all sufficient and good. We all need this reminder on a daily basis—and most of all when life is hard.

Look up Romans 8:18 in your favorite translation and write this short verse below:

Even if you are in Egypt right now, don't forget the promise that there is a Canaan. Though Jacob would die without seeing the promise fulfilled, he didn't doubt the certainty that there would be an exodus—and this surely gave him great comfort and hope.

Who in your life is really struggling right now? What is one way you can encourage this person with the truth that God is El Shaddai, the All-Sufficient One? Put a checkmark beside the action below that you will follow through with today.

Whatever you choose to do, remember not to downplay the person's pain. Just as Jacob acknowledged his pain to Pharaoh while clinging to the truth that God would fulfill every promise, you can be sensitive to the person's struggle while offering encouragement and hope.

_____ Send an encouraging text right now, including Romans 8:18 or another appropriate verse of Scripture.

_____ Post an encouraging message on social media, pointing out one of the person's good qualities.

_____ Call and say that even though he or she may be in Egypt (a foreign, uncomfortable place), there is the hope of Canaan—blessing. After validating the person's pain, share what you are learning from Genesis 48: that God's promises do not always follow human logic or tradition.

_____ Get out a pen, paper, envelope, and stamp and do the age-old snail mail thing. (Who doesn't love getting a personal note or letter in the midst of bills and advertisements?)

We must continually remind each other about God's goodness and His promise to bless us because life has a way of draining that truth right out of us. As we continue reading Genesis 48, we will find more truths about God's attributes and character.

Read Genesis 48:5-14 and number the events below in the order they occur in the text:

_____ Jacob celebrates the fact that he had the opportunity not only to see Joseph's face again but also to see Joseph's children.

_____ Jacob mentions the death of Joseph's mother, his beloved wife Rachel.

_____ Jacob crosses his arms so that he blesses the younger with the greater blessing.

_____ Jacob asks Joseph to bring the boys closer.

_____ Jacob adopts Ephraim and Manasseh as his own sons.

_____ Joseph positions the boys in front of Jacob and then bows before him, with his face to the ground.

Having reminded Joseph of God's promises to bless them (Genesis 48: 3-4), Jacob now prepares to bless his grandsons. His eyesight has grown dim, so he asks their father to confirm their identity as his grandsons. Surely Jacob has seen Ephraim and Manasseh many times previously during his seventeen years in Goshen. These boys are not toddlers sitting on his knees but young men in their early twenties. Next Jacob pronounces the blessing.

Read Genesis 48:15-16. What are some of the names of God Jacob uses in these verses?

Jacob refers to God as his Shepherd. A shepherd leads and cares for his sheep. He leaves the ninety-nine to pursue the lost sheep. Psalm 23:1-4 gives a beautiful picture of the kind of love and comfort Jacob is referring to here.

¹ The Lord is my shepherd;
  I have all that I need.
² He lets me rest in green meadows;
  he leads me beside peaceful streams.
³ He renews my strength.
He guides me along right paths,
  bringing honor to his name.
⁴ Even when I walk
  through the darkest valley,
I will not be afraid,
  for you are close beside me.
Your rod and your staff
  protect and comfort me. (Psalm 23:1-4)

Whether we are walking beside peaceful streams or through the darkest valley, our Good Shepherd cares for us and guides us along the right paths.

How has God been a Shepherd in your life recently?

Which of the phrases from Psalm 23:1-4 most resonates with you right now?

In addition to referring to God as his shepherd, Jacob refers to God as an Angel. Angels are created beings; they are God's messengers. Here Jacob is referring to God as the Messenger who spoke to him and redeemed him from all harm. These words are being spoken on his deathbed seventeen years after meeting Pharaoh and saying that he had had a hard life. Nearing the end of his life, Jacob possesses a clarity that those who are preoccupied with the stuff of this life sometimes overlook. I noticed this same quality in a beloved friend who died of brain cancer. In the last weeks of his life, he shared his life story with me, which was chock full of practical wisdom. I found that some of the simple truths he had shared with me came back to mind repeatedly in the months after he died. Here Jacob is blessing his family with the truth that God is his Shepherd and his Messenger.

As you look back on your journey to forgiveness these past six weeks, what messages has the Lord spoken to you? Recall any words of comfort, encouragement, or instruction, including specific Scriptures that He has used to speak to you personally. Flip through the pages of this workbook if you like, and make some notes below.

Now let's finish Genesis 48 by reading verses 17-22. What is Joseph upset about?

We know from verse 12 that Joseph is prostrate, with his face to the ground, as Jacob gives the blessing. It is from this position, after the blessing has already been given, that Joseph notices his father crossed his arms and gave his younger son priority over the older (vv. 17-18). I have to chuckle that Jacob does this, knowing that he himself stole the blessing from his older brother, Esau. However, Jacob isn't trying to be a stinker and root for the underdog. As one scholar points out, "Jacob may be losing his sight, but he is not losing his insight."[10] Remember that God is his Shepherd and Messenger and must have guided him in this prophetic hand switching.

I probably would have struggled with Jacob's hand crossing just as Joseph did. Considering what we see of Joseph through the Genesis narrative, my guess is that he was "type A" just like me. No matter what personality test I take, I come out with the words *systematic* or *detailed* on my profile. I like things that make sense, go in order, and fit neatly into flow charts. For Joseph to manage Potiphar's house, give oversight in the jail, and plan and execute the food program in Egypt, he had to be an organized list maker. (I don't know about you, but I love that about him.)

Another reason Joseph might have been so concerned about his father giving the greater blessing to the younger son would be his own circumstances. He might have been more sensitive because he had been the favored younger son and had seen the consequences of sibling rivalry. Perhaps he wanted to spare Ephraim and Manasseh any cause for enmity as brothers. Yet what seems most logical to us isn't always God's plan. Boy, have I found that to be true in my life. I have seen God work most mightily in the hardest of circumstances that I never would have chosen.

Joseph knew about receiving insight from God. Remember that Pharaoh asked Joseph to interpret his dream and Joseph said, "It is beyond my power to do this" (Genesis 41:16). He looked to God when coming out of the dungeon, but he favored tradition and logic when it came to his father blessing his boys. Like Joseph, sometimes we can struggle to trust when the revelation comes to another rather than directly to us. I tend to like to hear things for myself, but sometimes God chooses to speak to me through a trusted friend or adviser. Although He is a God of order, we need to remember that it is His order, not ours. His ways are perfect, but they don't always seem that way from our point of view.

What does Isaiah 55:9 (in the margin) say about God's ways and thoughts?

God's ways and thoughts transcend ours. We can't see the complete picture. If we could, we would make the same decision God would make. Knowing all the future generations in Ephraim and Manasseh's legacy, God let Jacob know that the younger would be greater than the older. This is not to say that order has no place.

> *For just as the heavens are higher than the earth,*
> *so my ways are higher than your ways*
> *and my thoughts higher than your thoughts.*
>
> *(Isaiah 55:9)*

> *Even when things go against what seems right to you, remember that God has a plan. And it's a perfect one!*

- God loves tradition. He instituted many rituals and celebrations (Leviticus 1).
- God loves logic; He is a God of order (1 Corinthians 14:33).

Even so, God is above both tradition and logic, and sometimes He leads us to go against these two general wisdoms. God wants us to live in close relationship with Him so that we may follow His ways.

In this study on forgiveness, we find one of the greatest truths that defies logic: *grace and mercy fly in the face of fairness*. Grace is amazing because it doesn't follow the pattern of sowing and reaping. We sin, and God forgives us, having paid the penalty for sin through the death of His own Son. It isn't fair; it is unmerited favor. Mercy is holding back the consequences of sin that we deserve. Romans 6:23 says, "For the wages of sin is death, but the free gift of God is eternal life through Christ Jesus our Lord." We deserve death, but out of His mercy God doesn't punish us. Then by His grace, He gives us a renewed relationship with Him and eternal life. So forgiveness employs both mercy and grace.

Contrary to popular belief, good people do not go to heaven; forgiven people do. That is the gospel message. And although this message engages both our heads and our hearts, faith is required in order for us to forgive others just as God has forgiven us. Forgiveness goes against our nature. It lives outside the logic box. But God says, *Don't follow the human logic of retribution or the fleshly feelings of bitterness; follow Me instead.*

Joseph believed his older son should receive the greater blessing, but God went against his human tradition and logic. Even when things go against what seems right to you, remember that God has a plan. And it's a perfect one!

We began today with Elizabeth's story of unexpected divorce. She would cry all the way to work and back home again, not understanding how divorce could be God's plan. Even though none of it made sense, she clung to God's Word, sought counseling, and relied on godly family and friends for encouragement and strength. Though she struggled for quite some time, she forgave her ex-husband and fixed her thoughts on the truths of God's commitment to her even in the famine of divorce. Looking back she can see so many blessings—things that God used for good in her life. She eventually remarried and had three amazing boys. She saw the Lord's mercy in so many details in a journey that she never would have chosen. It wasn't the story that made sense according to her logic, but God showed up in a huge way through her struggle. He promises to do the same for each of us!

Talk with God

Meditate on Hebrews 4:16: "So let us come boldly to the throne of our gracious God. There we will receive his mercy, and we will find grace to help us when we need it most." Come boldly before God and tell Him what is upsetting you right now—what is not going in order according to your plans. Lay it before the Shepherd who longs to care for you and lead you beside the still waters. Listen for the voice of the Messenger about what next steps He may have for you to take. Write anything you hear from Him in the margin.

Day 3: Legacy

While reading through First and Second Kings I was struck by the impact that our lives have on future generations. I thought about the legacy left to me. Though the family I grew up in was by no means perfect, my parents changed their family tree through their faith in Christ. They introduced their children to Jesus in a way that had not been modeled for either of them. I wrote them a letter at the time of my realization, thanking them for the legacy they left. This legacy included an environment where

- Jesus was talked about often.
- church was a huge part of our lives.
- VBS, church camps, retreats, and so many life-changing opportunities were made available and encouraged.
- all of us were challenged to think critically, questioning what we heard at church or school and seeking biblical truth for ourselves.

Before you think I had an idyllic childhood, let me say that I could make another list of some of the difficult times that would put that notion to rest. Suffice it to say that we were like every other family—imperfect.

Because our parents encouraged critical thinking, my siblings and I tend to question everything and love to argue. Sometimes we are contrary, and our family gatherings can be full of "spirited debates." However, when it comes to the stuff that matters most, I can say that my parents left us a legacy of Jesus. How about you?

What are three or four positive things that your parents left you as a legacy?

If it was hard to make this list, or if you didn't get much of a spiritual legacy, don't be discouraged. Jessica LaGrone points out in her Bible study *Broken and Blessed* (Abingdon Press: 2014) that Joseph followed God even when his brothers did not. She says that each of us can be the Joseph in our family tree. Even if no one else is following the Lord, you can stand alone and start a new legacy, influencing others for Christ.

As we turn to Genesis 49, we find Jacob's final blessings to his offspring. He adopted and blessed Joseph's two sons Ephraim and Manasseh in chapter 48; now he prophesies over the rest of his boys. These predictive words reveal different blessings or consequences for each of them.

Read through Genesis 49 and write a brief phrase or sentence about the prophesied future legacy of each son:

Son	Mother	Brief summary of the prophecy
Reuben	Leah	
Simeon and Levi	Leah	
Judah	Leah	
Zebulun	Leah	
Issachar	Leah	
Dan	Bilhah	
Gad	Zilpah	
Asher	Zilpah	
Naphtali	Bilhah	
Joseph	Rachel	
Benjamin	Rachel	

We see the fulfillment of many of these prophecies when we study the Israelite tribes in later biblical history. For example, the tribe of Zebulun did become seafaring people as Jacob mentioned. We also see the principle of sowing and reaping illustrated. Reuben, Simeon, and Levi left a legacy fraught with bad choices that would impact future generations of their family. One scholar observes, "From this first oracle the teaching is clear that the behavior of one individual affects the destiny of his descendants."[11]

How have you seen sin from one generation impact the next?

While tendencies toward anger, addiction, or other patterns of sin can trickle down from generation to generation, sin doesn't have to define us. We all have skeletons in our closet, but they don't have to be the legacy we leave.

As you look at the words Jacob spoke over Judah in verses 8-12, what sins from Judah's past are not mentioned here?

Let's not forget that Judah was a main character in the plot against young Joseph (Genesis 37). He also hired a prostitute, who, he later learned, was his daughter-in-law (Genesis 38). Yet throughout our study, we have seen a change in Judah. His heart is softer and his leadership is bolder; and now he is indicated as the lineage through which the Messiah will come. Jacob's pronouncement toward Judah is the second longest after the blessing of Joseph. Here in the blessing of Judah in verse 10 we find an obscure reference to a scepter. One scholar notes that the meaning of the Hebrew in this verse "is arguably the most debated in Genesis."[12] In college I was assigned a ten-page paper on this one verse!

Read Genesis 49:10 in the two different translations below. In each translation, underline the phrase that follows the word *until*.

The scepter shall not depart from Judah,
Nor a lawgiver from between his feet,
Until Shiloh comes;
And to Him shall be the obedience of the people. (NKJV)

The scepter will not depart from Judah,
    nor the ruler's staff from his descendants,
until the coming of the one to whom it belongs,
    the one whom all nations will honor. (NLT)

Some translations use the word *Shiloh* while others define *Shiloh* as "the one to whom it belongs," as we see above. Here are two opinions from scholars:

- "The name *Shiloh* in verse 10 has given rise to many interpretations and speculations, but the most reasonable is that it refers to the Messiah (Num. 24:17).[13]

- "The word 'Shiloh,' found in some English versions, is simply an untranslated form of the Hebrew expression meaning 'one to whom it belongs.'"[14]

Some see messianic promise here; others try to amend the text or make a connection to Judah's son Shelah. No matter what the exact meaning of Shiloh may be, we do know that Christ came through the line of Judah. Matthew 1:3 puts Judah as the son of Jacob in the lineage of Christ. Revelation 5:5 clearly refers to Christ in saying, "But one of the twenty-four elders said to me, 'Stop weeping! Look, the Lion of the tribe of Judah, the heir to David's throne, has won the victory. He is worthy to open the scroll and its seven seals.'" Even though the meaning of *Shiloh* is obscure in the Hebrew, we get to look from hindsight and see that Jacob was prophesying that the Messiah would come through the line of Judah.

Why didn't God use the line of Joseph rather than the line of Judah? Genesis records almost no flaws in Joseph's life but many in Judah's character. While we don't know the mind of God, it gives me hope to see God use greatly flawed people again and again for His eternal purposes. This shows us that God values repentance.

As you think about the sins you have struggled with in the past, how does knowing that the Messiah came through the line of Judah—not Joseph—motivate you to turn from your sin and toward God?

God wants to use us mightily in His kingdom plan, but we have a responsibility to repent. Let's look at two significant truths from the prophecies of Joseph's brothers.

1. We always have an opportunity to change direction.

Judah started out on the wrong road, but eventually he got back on the right path of yielding to God. We don't get a lot of scriptural details, but through our study we've seen the turning of Judah's life—with the culmination of it in Jacob's prophecy that Christ would be part of his lineage. If you have been walking in bitterness, resentment, or unforgiveness, you don't have to stay on that path!

We will never find peace by pursuing our own path over God's instructions. When we fail to practice forgiveness, we find ourselves driving off God's clearly marked roads onto rough and rocky ground that we weren't designed to travel. If we stubbornly refuse to obey, we might bottom out or have to dodge a few trees. However, like Judah, we can always pull back onto the paved path again. We still might hit some speed bumps when our old tendencies flare up, but we can slow down and depend on Christ to get us through.

2. Don't waste your suffering.

Joseph and Simeon both served unjust sentences in prison. Joseph learned through his sufferings, but Simeon did not. Living in an unfair world, we all have unique struggles. Many of them come at the hands of other people. The posture we take toward our suffering and our offenders will greatly affect the kind of character produced in our lives.

Considering this concept makes me want to grow through my trials and mistakes, learning to love my enemies so that I can fail forward. I don't want to waste a single tear or heartache. Wasting our sufferings by remaining hard-hearted and unteachable impacts the

The posture we take toward our suffering and our offenders will greatly affect the kind of character produced in our lives.

legacy we leave. If like Joseph and Judah we learn through our struggles, we can bestow blessing on the tribe that will come long after we have left this earth. Whether they are your children, nieces and nephews, kids in the Sunday school class you teach, teens you mentor, young moms you serve, or someone else you invest in, you are leaving a legacy to those who come after you.

Whether we waste our sufferings or gain insights through them has a ripple effect into the future. Genesis 49:7 reveals that Simeon—and Levi—created a negative ripple effect:

> *Cursed be their anger, for it is fierce;*
> *and their wrath, for it is cruel!*
> *I will divide them in Jacob*
> *and scatter them in Israel. (RSV)*

Commenting on this verse, one scholar writes, "Eventually Simeon is integrated into the tribe of Judah, and hence scatter here means 'dissolve.' "[15] In other words, Simeon's legacy dissolved into the tribe of Judah. Judah learned through suffering, and his legacy continued. Simeon wasted his suffering, and his tribe dissolved.

You are leaving a legacy. Is it one of forgiveness and attempted reconciliation, or is it one of hardness, bitterness, and pride? Obedience will bring blessing. We see this no clearer than in the blessing of Joseph.

Read Jacob's pronouncement over Joseph below (Genesis 49: 22-26 NIV). Underline every instance of the word *blessings*. Circle all of the names for God that you find.

> [22] *"Joseph is a fruitful vine,*
> *a fruitful vine near a spring,*
> *whose branches climb over a wall.*
> [23] *With bitterness archers attacked him;*
> *they shot at him with hostility.*
> [24] *But his bow remained steady,*
> *his strong arms stayed limber,*
> *because of the hand of the Mighty One of Jacob,*
> *because of the Shepherd, the Rock of Israel,*
> [25] *because of your father's God, who helps you,*
> *because of the Almighty, who blesses you*
> *with blessings of the skies above,*
> *blessings of the deep springs below,*
> *blessings of the breast and womb.*

²⁶ *Your father's blessings are greater*
   than the blessings of the ancient mountains,
   than the bounty of the age-old hills.
Let all these rest on the head of Joseph,
   on the brow of the prince among his brothers."

Joseph is the blessed prince among his brothers because he stayed on the path of intimacy with God. Throughout the Genesis account we've seen him relying on the Lord, forgiving his brothers, attributing any ability he has to God, and being used to save a nation through his good planning and insight. He left a legacy of blessings for those who came after him.

In these verses Jacob again calls God the Shepherd, and we see Almighty referring to El Shaddai, the All-Sufficient One. He also calls God a Rock.

How have you experienced God in these ways in your life?

Shepherd

All-Sufficient One

Rock

If someone were to interview the people with whom you have the closest contact on a regular basis, which would they say your legacy is more like?

_____ Judah: You had some pretty big mistakes in your past, but then you changed directions and began following God wholeheartedly.

_____ Simeon: You've suffered as much as anyone, but you continue to be led by your emotions rather than to learn from your past.

_____ Joseph: While nobody's perfect, you've lived a life of integrity, attempting to pursue God through times of difficulty and prosperity.

Most of us won't match any of these descriptions exactly since we all are unique and have different journeys. Yet these examples should prompt us to think about how our decisions today, tomorrow, and next week will shape the generations to come.

As we close today, prayerfully consider the traits that you would like to be representative of your life, inspiring those close to you. List three below:

1.

2.

3.

If we aim for nothing, we hit it every time. Identifying the legacy we would like to leave helps us set clearer goals. While none of us will do it perfectly, we can seek to leave a godly example.

Talk with God

Ask God to show you any changes He might want you to make related to the two main truths we explored today:

1. We always have an opportunity to change direction.
2. Don't waste your suffering.

Invite God to reveal any action steps He wants you to make in your thoughts, attitudes, or actions. Make notes in the margin of anything you hear.

Day 4: For Your Good

As I mentioned in the introduction, this Bible study was born out of my own struggle to forgive. I know all the Sunday school answers for why we should forgive. I have read God's commands to forgive many times and have recited the Lord's Prayer often. I understand that I am called to forgive my debtors. Of course, I have forgiven people on many occasions. We can't have families, coworkers, or friends and not have the need to forgive and be forgiven regularly.

Sinner + Sinner = Need for forgiveness often

Yet all of my prior experiences related to forgiveness were pebbles compared to this particular situation. It wasn't that something horrible had been done to me; it was that I had never before struggled so much to let go of offenses. I thought daily of the hurtful circumstances. I battled against old tapes that played in my head, reminding me of things that had been said or done. I read malicious intent into actions or inaction. The situation interrupted my dreams and invaded my thoughts and emotions. I found myself reading things on social media and making assumptions. I couldn't wrap my mind around what had happened to change the lenses we saw each other through. Once we had believed the best and encouraged each other, but now everything was awkward and uncomfortable. Being an unforgiving stalker can be exhausting, and I wanted to just get over it. In my heart I wanted to forgive as Joseph forgave, but my thoughts and emotions weren't following my desire to let it go. Every day I wasted mental energy trying to make sense of the situation, looking for answers as to why it happened, how I played a part in it, and if I should leave it alone after several failed attempts at relationship repair. I didn't know why I couldn't just will myself to obey Jesus' clear command, "Forgive, and you will be forgiven" (Luke 6:37 NIV). I wanted to do that, but it proved more difficult than it sounded.

I prayed. I journaled. I studied and memorized Scripture. By studying Joseph's life, I hoped to unlock the secret of his powerful journey to forgiveness. How did he do it?

In preparation for writing this study, I read not only the Genesis commentaries but also many different books on the topic of forgiveness (which you'll find listed at the back of this book). I gleaned many helpful insights and truths along the way. But it was in the final portion of the Joseph saga, which we are studying today, where I found the most beneficial truth of all on my personal journey to forgiveness. Isn't it just like God to save the best for last? What we will discover today is this: forgiveness takes our initiative and faith but comes only through the great Forgiver.

By believing that God had a sovereign plan, Joseph learned to let go of the why and get to the *what* in his life. Early in his journey he never could have understood why

- God gave him dreams.
- His brothers sold him.
- Potiphar promoted him and then Potiphar's wife unjustly accused him.
- He languished in prison for years.

Only later could he put the pieces together and see God working through it all—even if he didn't fully understand. We've seen him wrestle with grace and test the boundaries of trust. He didn't get stuck in his journey, though. He moved forward until he got to the

Fun Fact:

"Although Jesus by birth was of the tribe of Judah, through his residence in Nazareth he was of the tribe of Zebulon by domicile. The Gospels record Jesus' interest in ships and fishing, and the body of water on which he fished is the same body of water with which the Zebulonites are associated here in the Blessing of Jacob." [16]

Forgiveness takes our initiative and faith but comes only through the great Forgiver.

point where he could fully embrace and continually practice forgiveness toward his offenders. He also pursued reconciliation with boundaries to find a new normal in his relationships with his brothers.

I often struggle to let go of the *why*. I want to know immediately the purpose of my pain instead of setting my eyes on how I can learn and grow through the journey.

How about you? Which one of these thoughts most closely matches your circumstances right now?

_____ I'm not struggling to figure out the *why* in anything in my life right now.

_____ I occasionally wonder why things are happening, but not very often.

_____ Almost every day I contemplate why this particular situation is happening in my life. I want to release it and trust God, but I'm struggling.

As a human being, Joseph probably wondered why things were happening in his life, but he learned to trust God and move forward through both the good and bad times.

Turn to Genesis 50. Read verses 1-13, and summarize what happens after Jacob blesses all of his sons:

Joseph honors his father's request, and the family mourns Jacob's death together in the land of their childhood.

Note on the map to the right how close the Cave of Machpelah (where they buried Jacob) is to Dothan (where Joseph's brothers sold him into slavery) by drawing a line between them.

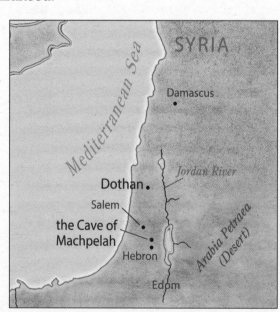

For the first time since he was seventeen, Joseph retraced the steps that he took when his brothers first sold him. Though he probably didn't travel all the way to Dothan to look into the pit where his brothers held him against his will, he likely recalled the journey between Egypt and his homeland. Along the way, he would have encountered the terrain and landmarks that he stumbled across while he was bound by Ishmaelite traders. No doubt this experience would have triggered painful memories in his heart and mind.

Have you ever revisited a place that evoked painful memories for you?

It's not right or wrong to have these memories. If visiting a place of pain causes hurt to resurface, that does not necessarily mean we haven't forgiven. Often it simply means that something hurt us and we remember it. Where the rubber meets the road on our forgiveness journeys is what we do with that pain. From what perspective will we choose to view the past? Where will we focus our minds and hearts? Will we continue to see God's blessings through the harm done to us and trust Him, or will we allow our hearts to harden with thoughts of retribution?

Though we do not know for certain if this trip caused any painful memories to resurface for Joseph, we do know that his brothers began to remember their sins against him.

Read Genesis 50:14-21. Let's walk through this climax of our story step by step.

What do Joseph's brothers begin to worry about when they return home to Goshen after mourning the death of their father in Canaan? (v. 15)

What emotion would you say motivates the brothers to send a message to Joseph?

These boys are again walking in fear. Unresolved guilt can endure for years and lead us to fear. Rather than confessing and releasing to God the wrongs from their past, these brothers seem to be holding on to their guilt.

We often suspect others of what we know our tendency might be in a situation. Perhaps the brothers are thinking that if they were in Joseph's shoes, seeing Canaan would stir up thoughts of getting even. One commentator writes, "Joseph has given them no premonition or reason to think that his spirit is retaliatory, that he has been laying low and waiting for the most propitious moment for vengeance. This, incidentally, is the first time that the brothers acknowledge their guilt for what they did to Joseph."[17]

What message do the brothers send to Joseph? (vv. 16-17)

Do you think Jacob really gave them this message before he died? Why or why not?

Though the text doesn't say definitively whether Jacob gave the brothers this message, it would be strange for him to leave the message with them instead of with Joseph himself. Jacob had plenty of opportunity to give Joseph the message when he asked Joseph to promise to bury him in his homeland; at that time he could have added that he wanted Joseph to go easy on his brothers. In my opinion, it seems that the boys are up to their old tricks, manipulating circumstances instead of trusting God. Oh, I want to scold them self-righteously—except for the ring of conviction in my own life.

What are some ways you have you resorted to manipulating circumstances instead of trusting God?

I've thought of some habitual patterns of manipulation in my own life that are not easy to admit:

- In my marriage, I have a tendency to nag instead of pray.
- I sometimes justify buying something that I know I can't afford.

- In conversation, I occasionally drop hints about something I want to happen, hoping others will jump on my bandwagon.

We follow a long line of biblical men and women who practiced manipulation from time to time. Abraham lied to Pharaoh about Sarah being his wife, fearing that her beauty might put him in danger (Genesis 12). Rebekah feared that her son Jacob wouldn't get the blessing God promised, so she decided to help God out by manipulating her blind husband, Isaac (Genesis 27). And here in Genesis 50 we have the likely manipulation of Joseph by his fearful brothers. We would be wise to consider their example the next time we are tempted to orchestrate events or tell lies in an attempt to assuage our fears.

What was Joseph's reaction to his brothers' message? (v. 17)

Why do you think he reacted this way?

I wonder if Joseph's heartbreak is due to the fact that his brothers still don't get it. Rather than turn to the Shepherd, the Rock, the Messenger, the All-Sufficient One who has power over all things, they continue to make decisions based in fear. After all this time, his brothers haven't learned to trust God.

When have you felt the heartbreak of watching those you love choose to live in fear instead of trusting God?

Another possible cause for Joseph's tears could be his brothers' doubt about his sincerity. They are essentially questioning his character and integrity. Whether Joseph sent for them or they came on their own accord, verse 18 reveals that the brothers threw themselves down before Joseph, offering to be his slaves. Living in fear instead of faith shackles us in self-inflicted servitude.

My long process of forgiveness left me paralyzed, wasting time I could have spent praying, appreciating blessings, and loving others. I was so consumed with the *why* when God was calling me to see His hand working for good even in the midst of painful circumstances.

Despite his brothers' doubts, Joseph could see through the clear lenses of his "God glasses" to love and bless them.

> *And we know that in all things God works for the good of those who love him, who have been called according to his purpose.*
>
> *(Romans 8:28 NIV)*

This verse is the theme of the entire Joseph saga. When we walk in fear, bitterness, cynicism, or resentment, refusing to forgive or consider reconciliation, we miss seeing how God wants to take even the situations that others intended for our harm and use them for good in our lives. He also wants to use us as His conduit to bless others. Our part is to trust and obey. It sounds simple, but we all know it is a journey rather than a destination.

We will not "arrive" at total trust in God until we are standing face-to-face with Him, removed from the very presence of sin in heaven. Until that day, like Joseph, we might suffer through intense betrayals, separation from those we love, temptations put before us by others, and dungeon days where it's difficult to trust and obey. Referring to Genesis 50:20, Stuart Briscoe writes, "To say this is one thing. To believe it in theory is another. But to relentlessly hold to it in the dark days of betrayal and the lonely years in prison is faith of the highest order."[18] Joseph shows us that it is possible to live out the truth of this verse through the highs and lows of life.

Genesis 50:20 is often referred to as the Romans 8:28 of the Old Testament.

Joseph's brothers meant harm toward him when they sold him. But God worked it for good.

The concept of God working all things for good is the key to moving forward in forgiveness.

For me, the concept of God working all things for good is the key to moving forward in forgiveness. When I get stuck, focusing on offenses, I neglect to see all the amazing things God has given me through them. I must lay down the *why* and ask *what*:

- God, what can I do to be used by You through this situation to benefit others?
- Lord, what can I learn through my pain?
- Father, what implications will my choices have in the legacy I leave for others?

Read Through Joseph's Family Story: Read Genesis 48.

Note that every one of these questions begins with God's name. When bad things happen, our nature is to default to why. But God calls us to shift our focus to Him and His greater plan, even when people do hurtful things.

Here are some of the things I've found that can be helpful on the journey to forgiveness:

- When old wounds threaten to resurface, redirect your thoughts to the blessings that come from the conflict.
- When you are in need of healing, hide people from your social media feeds if necessary to keep you from the temptations of making assumptions, feeling jealous, or missing what used to be.
- When a negative thought or memory pops into your head, pray blessings over those involved.
- Purposely speak well of those who hurt you to others.
- When you encounter those who hurt you, look for ways to bless them by smiling or initiating conversation.

What are some other practical ideas you can implement the next time you start to focus on your losses instead of the gains God can give you through a conflict?

Joseph's grace-filled response to his brothers flowed from years of making secret heart choices. Through many years of praying, testing, and trusting God's ways over the tendencies of his flesh, Joseph moved forward in forgiveness. He persevered on God's path of grace, looking for a greater purpose and plan. You can move forward in forgiveness too. As you build endurance through your own trials, God will grow you in His grace.

Talk with God

Meditate again on Genesis 50:20 and Romans 8:28. Thank God that He uses for good what others mean for harm in our lives. Ask God to help you believe the truth of these verses, especially when you can't see even one benefit in the midst of your pain. Pray also for God to transform your heart so that you can trust He is working things together for greater purposes in the midst of your forgiveness story.

As you seek to reconcile the conflict between the way that you feel and the truth of what God says, I pray God's voice will win out in your heart and mind. He wants to take the "all things" going on in your life right now and use them as ingredients to make something amazing with your life.

Day 5: Staying the Course

How can we be at the end of our journey through Joseph's story of forgiveness? The Book of Genesis chronicles the beginnings of the people of Israel. For generations this family will be referred to by the name of Joseph's father, Jacob, renamed Israel by God (Genesis 35:10). They will make a grand exodus from the land of Egypt through the leadership of Moses. A journey to the Promised Land will be filled with all sorts of lessons on fear and discontent as they wander for forty years before reaching their destination. Later they will be led by judges and then kings. Truly our ending point is only the first leg of the trip for the tribes of Israel.

Read Genesis 50:22-26 and answer the following questions:

How many years did Joseph live?

How many generations did he live to see and enjoy?

In Joseph's final words to his brothers, we find a deathbed encouragement and a request. In your own words, write what he says to reassure them in verse 24:

As I think about these verses where Joseph comforts his brothers by saying that God will come to help them, I wonder if life has already begun to get difficult for them in Goshen. As the years have gone by and they have multiplied and prospered, are the Egyptians already beginning to fear their numbers? Regardless, Joseph spends his last words reminding the brothers of God's truth and encouraging them to keep believing. God faithfully uses people, His Word, and all sorts of methods to remind us that

He can be trusted. Today, remember that although His timing may not be yours, God will keep every promise He has made to you. The exodus from Egypt would not begin for three more centuries after Joseph's death, but God did bring His people home.

What was Joseph's request according to verse 25?

Joseph follows his father's example of wanting his eventual resting place to be the land of Canaan. However, he does not ask his brothers to take his body back right away and mourn for him as they did for Jacob. Instead, he wants his coffin to serve as a memorial to the future fulfillment of God's promise. He refers to his body as *bones*, knowing that the return to Canaan will not be immediate. Even in death, Joseph wants to remind others to trust God. His journey of forgiveness ends with him encouraging the growth of their faith with his own body. Many scholars refer to Joseph as a Christ type because of the many parallels between the two. Certainly, Christ offered up His own body to do much more than encourage our faith—*to save our very souls.*

The descendants of these twelve brothers would later be the very ones who would make false accusations and betray the Messiah that God sent to rescue them. Nowhere do we see Genesis 50:20 lived out more clearly than in the Crucifixion. They surely meant to harm Jesus, but God always intended to use it all for good so that we could be saved. As He suffered on the cross, Jesus uttered these words: "Father, forgive them, for they don't know what they are doing" (Luke 23:34).

The horrible betrayal that Judas issued with a kiss led to Jesus' arrest, mocking, whipping, a crown of thorns, and an indescribable death on a cross. Without the sovereign plan of God, this would seem like a senseless travesty with no silver lining at all. Yet we know that God used what others meant for harm for the ultimate, greatest good. Because of this betrayal, we have the opportunity to be saved.

Take a moment to read the following verses that so wonderfully remind us why Christ died for us on the cross:

For everyone has sinned; we all fall short of God's glorious standard. (Romans 3:23)

But God showed his great love for us by sending Christ to die for us while we were still sinners. (Romans 5:8)

If you openly declare that Jesus is Lord and believe in your heart that God raised him from the dead, you will be saved. (Romans 10:9)

Fun Fact:
"Every one says forgiveness is a lovely idea, until they have something to forgive."[19]
—C. S. Lewis, Mere Christianity

But to all who believed him and accepted him, he gave the right to become children of God. (John 1:12)

How do these verses about Christ illustrate the truth of Genesis 50:20—that what others mean for harm God will use for good?

Forgiveness is like breathing. We inhale Christ's forgiveness for us, and then we exhale forgiveness toward others.

One of the gals in my Bible study group used this illustration to talk about forgiveness. Forgiveness is like breathing. We inhale Christ's forgiveness for us, and then we exhale forgiveness toward others. So, the more we inhale or accept Christ's amazing grace for us, the more we are able to exhale or extend forgiveness to others.

How has inhaling (accepting) Christ's forgiveness for you helped you exhale (extend) forgiveness to others?

Joseph breathed very deeply of God's goodness in the midst of trials. Then he exhaled that forgiveness onto the betrayers in his life, believing that God had more power than they did. He refused to accept that mere humans could stomp out God-given dreams. The ironic thing is that his brothers' attempt to kill his dreams unknowingly advanced them instead.

People may be trying to hurt you, but unknowingly they might be putting you in a place where God's dreams for you can be fulfilled. They might be the sandpaper that helps to smooth your edges. Perhaps they will move you down a necessary road you never would have taken on your own. If you can see beyond the pain they are causing you to God's ability to work out a greater plan, you can begin to see their arrows as opportunities that God can use to bring blessing and fulfill His dreams for your life.

As we come to the close of our study, we press on in our pursuit of forgiveness. We ask for Joseph's perspective to trust God's greater plan through the daily ups and downs of life. We ask for forgiveness like daily food or even the very breaths that we breathe. Let's end our time together with a short review of what we've learned through Joseph's journey to forgiveness.

Read Acts 7:9-18 for a short recap of Joseph's life as told by Stephen. Record any elements in this retelling that especially resonate with you:

Joseph's journey to forgiveness was a marathon, not a sprint. As you look back over our six weeks together by reading this chart, reflect on the questions below and ask God to make clear which week of study is most relevant to your life right now.

Week of Study	Main Concept	Reflection Questions
1. Acknowledging the Pain (Genesis 37, 39)	We saw the brothers hurting because of favoritism, but they poured gasoline on the fire of their pain instead of God's water of forgiveness.	Is there a spark of conflict in your life? Will you fuel the fire or seek God's help to extinguish the flames before it burns out of control?
2. Waiting to Be Remembered (Genesis 40)	Through his dark days in prison, Joseph practiced discernment in the midst of the haze of his circumstances and clung to his dreams, even when he couldn't see a possibility of fulfillment.	Are you in a season of waiting? Even when you feel stuck, will you continue to cling to God's promise to bless you? During times of testing, will you allow God to develop your character?
3. Dreams Coming True (Genesis 41–42)	God blessed Joseph in the land of his suffering. He maintained his integrity, work ethic, and trust in God as he gained position, power, and a new family.	Are you coming out of a time of testing and experiencing circumstantial favor? How can you keep from forgetting God now that the desperation of trials is not driving you toward Him?
4. The Roller Coaster Ride (Genesis 43–44)	Joseph encountered his brothers again and put them through a series of tests to see if they were safe for reestablishing trust. Joseph tested before he trusted.	Does life feel like it's up one day and down the next? Have you come to a place of forgiveness in your heart, but you aren't sure if God is calling you to pursue reconciliation?
5. Grace and Boundaries (Genesis 45–46)	Joseph blessed his brothers but didn't move in next door to them. He pursued peace, provided blessings instead of retribution, and exercised some boundaries so they could find a new normal in their relationship.	Are you reconnecting with someone after a recent or long-standing conflict? What can you do to intentionally bless this person but also navigate the proper boundaries to promote healing so past mistakes aren't repeated?
6. Moving Forward (Genesis 47–50)	Until his dying day, Joseph encouraged his brothers to seek God. He forgave them fully and wanted them to understand that what they meant for harm, God used for the good of them all.	How can you see God's hand in the midst of the harm caused by others? Will you hold firmly to God's promise to work everything together for your good?

Draw a big star next to the week of study that is most relevant to you today. How does that portion of Joseph's story echo into your current circumstances?

Now take a moment to write a few short responses to the reflection questions for the week of study you selected (right column):

God has had me on a roller coaster for quite some time. As our study closes, I see God transforming my heart and mind as I breathe in His grace and then exhale forgiveness toward others. I wouldn't trade any of the pain for the amazing lessons I've learned. I don't know if I could have said that with honesty six months ago. Isn't God good!

Joseph has reminded me how intimately God is involved in all the details of the conflicts we experience and how He uses them to bring blessing in our lives. Joseph stands out in sharp contrast not only to his brothers but also to the average Christian. We talk a good forgiveness game, but Joseph demonstrated it with his life. He was surrounded by pagan religions on all sides and had no encouragement from fellow believers or even a physical copy of God's Word to sustain him. When we think of our excuses for not following God into the land of forgiveness, it is humbling to know that Joseph stayed the course.

Until the day he died, Joseph believed God's promises would come true. In fact, of all the good things we saw in Joseph's life, it was his persevering hope on his deathbed that gained him mention in the Hebrews 11 hall of faith: "It was by faith that Joseph, when he was about to die, said confidently that the people of Israel would leave Egypt. He even commanded them to take his bones with them when they left" (v. 22). It was this confident faith in God that allowed Joseph to

- persevere under hardship.
- forgive his betrayers.
- pursue reconciliation.
- believe God's promises to bring them out of Egypt.

Like Joseph, we can breathe forgiveness out only when we have fully embraced it for ourselves from a most gracious God. I don't know where you are on your journey to forgiveness, but I pray that the Genesis account of Joseph's life has inspired you to believe God and release any bitterness, resentment, or unforgiveness that has been weighing you down. Sweet freedom is waiting!

Talk with God

Take some time right now to listen in God's presence. Ask:

- Have I fully embraced the forgiveness You purchased on the cross to set me free?
- Is there someone I haven't fully forgiven?
- Are you asking me to pursue reconciliation in any estranged relationships?

After prayerfully considering these questions in His presence, write a prayer in the margin expressing your desire to believe His promises and live in obedience to His command to forgive.

Rest assured that no matter what you've endured, God won't waste a bit of it. He longs to be your All-Sufficient One as well as your Shepherd, Rock, Messenger, and Angel—just as He was for Jacob and Joseph. No matter what you may face in the coming weeks and months, remember that God promises to use it all for good!

Read Through Joseph's Family Story:

Read Genesis 49–50.

Digging Deeper

Though Joseph was a sinner just like you and me, his life contains many hints that foreshadow the coming of a future Savior. Check out the Digging Deeper article for Week 6, "Messianic Glimpses," to learn more about the correlations between Joseph and Jesus (see AbingdonPress.com/Joseph).

Moving Forward

God's plan doesn't always follow _____ and

_____.

Even in the midst of conflict, God calls us to give an _____

_____.

We have to stay the course of reconciliation instead of retribution even when

people _____ _____.

But now that their father was dead, Joseph's brothers became fearful. "Now Joseph will show his anger and pay us back for all the wrong we did to him," they said.

So they sent this message to Joseph: "Before your father died, he instructed us to say to you: 'Please forgive your brothers for the great wrong they did to you—for their sin in treating you so cruelly.' So we, the servants of the God of your father, beg you to forgive our sin." When Joseph received the message, he broke down and wept. Then his brothers came and threw themselves down before Joseph. "Look, we are your slaves!" they said. (Genesis 50:15-18)

VIDEO VIEWER GUIDE: WEEK 6

"You have heard the law that says, 'Love your neighbor' and hate your enemy. But I say, love your enemies! Pray for those who persecute you! In that way, you will be acting as true children of your Father in heaven. For he gives his sunlight to both the evil and the good, and he sends rain on the just and the unjust alike. If you love only those who love you, what reward is there for that? Even corrupt tax collectors do that much. If you are kind only to your friends, how are you different from anyone else? Even pagans do that." (Matthew 5:43-47)

But Joseph replied, "Don't be afraid of me. Am I God, that I can punish you? You intended to harm me, but God intended it _____ for _____. He brought me to this position so I could save the lives of many people." (Genesis 50:19-20)

Genesis 50:20 is often referred to as the _____ of the Old Testament.

And we know that in all things God works for the good of those who love him, who have been called according to his purpose. (Romans 8:28 NIV)

RECOMMENDED READING

If you would like to explore the topic of forgiveness in more depth, these are my recommendations (in order):

1. *Forgive and Forget: Healing the Hurts We Don't Deserve*, Lewis B. Smedes (New York: HarperCollins, 1984)
2. *Forgiveness: Finding Peace through Letting Go*, Adam Hamiliton (Nashville: Abingdon Press, 2012)
3. *The Art of Forgiving: When You Need to Forgive and Don't Know How*, Lewis B. Smedes (New York: Ballantine Books,1996)
4. *Mere Christianity*, C. S. Lewis (New York: HarperCollins, 2001)
5. *What's So Amazing About Grace*, Philip Yancey (Grand Rapids: Zondervan, 1997)
6. *Forgiving As We've Been Forgiven: Community Practices for Making Peace*, L. Gregory Jones and Celestin Musekura (Downer's Grove: InterVarsity, 2010)
7. *Forgiveness: Following Jesus into Radical Loving*, Paula Huston (Brewster, MA: Paraclete Press, 2008)
8. *Forgiveness: Overcoming the Impossible*, Matthew West (Nashville: Thomas Nelson, 2013)
9. *How Can I Possibly Forgive: Rescuing Your Heart from Resentment and Regret*, Sara Horn (Eugene, OR: Harvest House Publishers, 2014)
10. *Choosing Forgiveness: Your Journey to Freedom*, Nancy Leigh DeMoss (Chicago: Moody Publishers, 2006)
11. *Radical Forgiveness: It's Time to Wipe Your Slate Clean!*, Julie Ann Barnhill (Carol Stream, IL: Tyndale House Publishers, 2004)

These books are either fictional or real accounts of forgiveness (again in recommended order):

1. *Joseph*, Terri L. Fivash (Hagerstown, MD: Review & Herald Publishing, 2002)
2. *Unbroken: A World War II Story of Survival, Resilience, and Redemption*, Laura Hillenbrand (New York: Random House, 2014)
3. *The Hiding Place*, Corrie Ten Boom (Grand Rapids: Chosen Books, 2006)
4. *The Sunflower*, Simon Wiesenthal (New York: Schocken Books, 1997)

NOTES

Week 1

1. Frank E. Gaebelein, general editor, *The Expositor's Bible Commentary Volume 2* (Grand Rapids: Zondervan, 1990), 227.
2. Henry M. Morris, *The Genesis Record: A Scientific and Devotional Commentary on the Book of Beginnings* (Grand Rapids: Baker, 1976), 536.
3. Warren W. Wiersbe, *Be Authentic: Exhibiting Real Faith in the Real World: OT Commentary, Genesis 25–50* (Colorado Springs: David C. Cook, 1997), 95.
4. Lewis B, Smedes, *Forgive and Forget: Healing the Hurts We Don't Deserve* (New York: HarperCollins, 1984), 2.
5. Ibid.
6. Lewis B. Smedes, *The Art of Forgiving: When You Need to Forgive and Don't Know How* (New York: Ballantine Books,1996), 4.
7. Morris, 541.
8. Walter Brueggemann, *Genesis: Interpretation: A Bible Commentary for Teaching and Preaching* (Louisville: John Knox Press, 1982), 305.
9. Gaebelein, 234.
10. Wiersbe, 107.
11. Morris, 559.
12. Wiersbe, 109.

Week 2

1. Jack Canfield, *The Success Principles: How to Get from Where You Are to Where You Want to Be* (New York: HarperCollins, 2005), 6.
2. Nancy Leigh DeMoss, *Choosing Forgiveness: Your Journey to Freedom* (Chicago: Moody Publishers, 2006), 128.
3. Smedes, *Forgive and Forget*, 44.
4. Brueggemann, 324.
5. Smedes, *The Art of Forgiving*, 5.
6. Ibid, 6.
7. Paula Huston, *Forgiveness: Following Jesus into Radical Loving* (Brewster: Paraclete Press, 2008), 99.
8. Adam Hamilton, *Forgiveness: Finding Peace Through Letting Go* (Nashville: Abingdon Press, 2012), 14.
9. Ibid.
10. Leighann McCoy, *Spiritual Warfare for Women: Winning the Battle for Your Home, Family, and Friends* (Minneapolis: Bethany House, 2011), 143.
11. Ibid, 179.
12. A. Hamilton, 14.
13. Ibid, 119-120.
14. Smedes, *Forgive and Forget*, xvii-xix.

Week 3

1. Wiersbe, 107.
2. Ibid, 111.
3. D. Stuart Briscoe, *Genesis: The Preacher's Commentary Vol. 1,* Lloyd J. Ogilvie, general editor (Nashville: Thomas Nelson, 2004), 321.
4. Brueggemann, 326.
5. Briscoe, 322.
6. Brueggemann, 331.
7. Wiersbe, 122.

8. Briscoe, 330.

9. Dee Brestin, *Friendships of Women: The Beauty and Power of God's Plan for Us* (Colorado Springs: David C. Cook, 2008), 175-76.

10. Ibid, 183.

11. Brueggemann, 337.

12. *Bachan*, http://www.blbclassic.org/lang/lexicon/lexicon.cfm?Strongs=H974&t=NASB.

13. Victor P. Hamilton, *The Book of Genesis Chapters 18–50 – The New International Version Commentary on the Old Testament*, (Grand Rapids: William B. Eerdmans Publishing Company, 1995), 522.

14. Ibid.

Week 4

1. *Nasâ*, http://www.biblestudytools.com/lexicons/hebrew/nas/nasa.html.

2. V. Hamilton, 539.

3. Wiersbe, 130.

4. Brueggemann, 339.

5. *El Shaddai*, https://www.blueletterbible.org/study/misc/name_god.cfm.

6. V. Hamilton, 541.

7. Bruce K. Waltke, *Genesis: A Commentary* (Grand Rapids: Zondervan, 2001), 550.

8. Charles F. Aling, *Egypt and Bible History: From Earliest Times to 1000 B.C.* (Grand Rapids: Baker, 1981), 99.

9. Gaebelein, 251.

10. V. Hamilton, 550.

11. Wiersbe, 132.

12. V. Hamilton, 556.

13. Philip Yancey, *What's So Amazing About Grace?* (Grand Rapids: Zondervan, 1997), 90.

14. V. Hamilton, 559.

15. Yancey, 84–85.

16. Ibid, 85.

17. Smedes, *The Art of Forgiving*, xi–xii.

18. Wiersbe, 140.

19. Gaebelein, 253.

20. V. Hamilton, 564.

21. Waltke, 566.

22. Smedes, *The Art of Forgiving*, 26.

23. Ibid, 56.

24. C.S. Lewis, *The Weight of Glory* (New York: HarperCollins, 2001), 182.

25. Smedes, *The Art of Forgiving*, 27.

26. Waltke, 550.

Week 5

1. Waltke, 562.

2. Matthew West, *Forgiveness: Overcoming the Impossible* (Nashville: Thomas Nelson, 2013), 3, 5.

3. Waltke, 562.

4. Smedes, Forgive and Forget, 32.

5. Ibid, 32–34.

6. Ibid., 33.

7. Weirsbe, 144.

8. L. Gregory Jones and Celestin Musekura, *Forgiving As We've Been Forgiven: Community Practices for Making Peace* (Downer's Grove: InterVarsity, 2010), 28.

9. V. Hamilton, 575.

10. Wiersbe, 144.
11. Jones and Musekura, 27.
12. *Condensed Biblical Encyclopedia*, "Joseph," http://www.biblestudytools.com/encyclopedias/condensed-biblical-encyclopedia/joseph.html.
13. Corrie Ten Boom, *The Hiding Place* (Grand Rapids: Chosen Books, 1984), 246-47.
14. Wiersbe, 146.
15. Ibid.
16. Henry Cloud and John Townsend, *Boundaries: When to Say Yes, How to Say No to Take Control of Your Life* (Grand Rapids: Zondervan, 1992), 42.
17. DeMoss, 194.
18. Cloud and Townsend, i.
19. Waltke, 572.
20. Cloud and Townsend, 31.
21. Wiersbe, 154.
22. Serenity Prayer, commonly attributed to Reinhold Neibuhr. http://www.thevoiceforlove.com/serenity-prayer.html; http://www.nytimes.com/2008/07/11/us/11prayer.html?_r=0.
23. V. Hamilton, 589.

Week 6

1. V. Hamilton, 606.
2. Waltke, 586.
3. V. Hamilton, 607.
4. Waltke, 587.
5. *Maguwr,* http://www.biblestudytools.com/lexicons/hebrew/nas/maguwr.html.
6. Wiersbe, 156.
7. Briscoe, 366.
8. Ibid, 367.
9. Wiersbe, 160.
10. V. Hamilton, 636.
11. Ibid, 647.
12. Waltke, 608.
13. Wiersbe, 166.
14. Gaebelein, 276.
15. V. Hamilton, 652.
16. Ibid., 664.
17. Ibid, 702.
18. Briscoe, 392.
19. C. S. Lewis, *Mere Christianity* (New York: HarperCollins, 2001), 115.

Meet Our Abingdon Women Authors

Jessica LaGrone is Dean of the Chapel at Asbury Theological Seminary and an acclaimed pastor, teacher, and speaker who enjoys leading retreats and events throughout the United States. She previously served as Pastor of Creative Ministries at The Woodlands UMC in Houston, Texas. She is the author of _Namesake: When God Rewrites Your Story, Broken and Blessed: How God Changed the World Through One Imperfect Family,_ and _Set Apart: Holy Habits of Prophets and Kings_. She and her husband, Jim, have two young children. For speaking and booking information and to follow her blog, Reverend Mother, visit jessicalagrone.com.

Babbie Mason is an award-winning singer and songwriter; a women's conference speaker; a leader of worship celebration-concerts for women; adjunct professor of songwriting at Lee University; and television talk-show host of _Babbie's House_. She has led worship for national and international events hosted by Billy Graham, Charles Stanley, Anne Graham Lotz, Women of Faith, and others. She is the author of _Embraced by God_ and _This I Know for Sure_. For information about speaking and events, visit babbie.com.

Kimberly Dunnam Reisman is known for her effective and engaging preaching and teaching. Kim is the World Director of World Methodist Evangelism and has served as the Executive Director of Next Step Evangelism Ministries and Adjunct Professor at United Theological Seminary. Kim is the author or co-author of numerous books and studies, including _The Christ-Centered Woman: Finding Balance in a World of Extremes._ The mother of three adult children, Kim and her husband live in West Lafayette, Indiana. For information about speaking and events, visit kimberlyreisman.com.

Melissa Spoelstra is a popular women's conference speaker, Bible teacher, and writer who is passionate about helping other women to seek Christ and know Him more intimately through serious Bible study. In addition to _Joseph: The Journey to Forgiveness,_ she is the author of _Jeremiah: Daring to Hope in an Unstable World_. She lives in Dublin, Ohio, with her pastor husband and four kids. For events and booking information and to follow her blog, visit MelissaSpoelstra.com.

Cindi Wood is a sought-after speaker and Bible teacher with events throughout the United States and abroad. Through biblically-based teaching coupled with humor from daily experience, Cindi offers hope and encouragement to women of all ages and walks of life. She is the author of numerous books and Bible studies, including _Anonymous: Discovering the Somebody You Are to God_ and the Frazzled Female Series. Cindi lives in Kings Mountain, North Carolina with her husband, Larry. For events and booking information, visit FrazzledFemale.com.

Learn more at AbingdonWomen.com.